Matisse, His Art and His Textiles

The Fabric of Dreams

Man Ray, Henri Matisse
with model, 1928.
Photograph

Matisse, His Art and His Textiles

The Fabric of Dreams

ROYAL ACADEMY OF ARTS

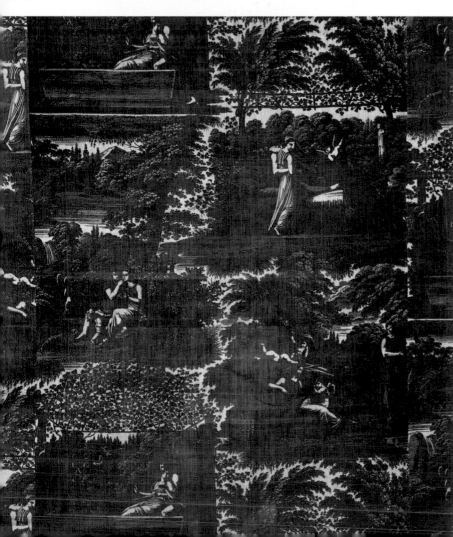

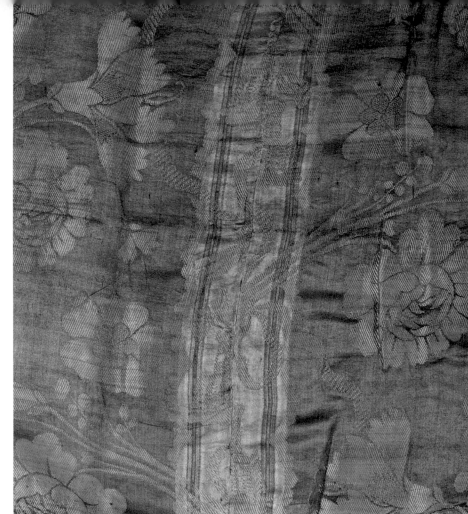

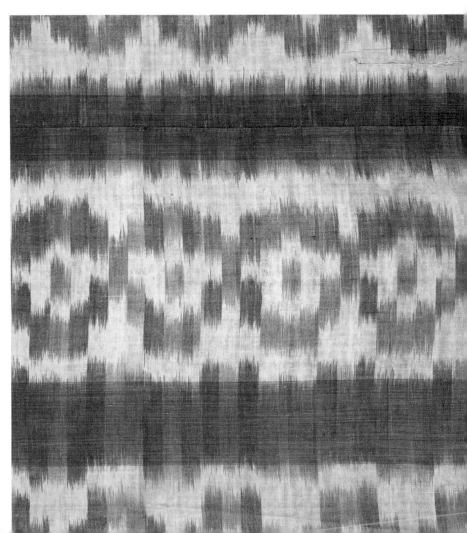

First published on the occasion of the exhibition
**Matisse, His Art and His Textiles:
The Fabric of Dreams**

Musée Matisse, Le Cateau-Cambrésis
23 October 2004 – 25 January 2005

The Jillian and Arthur M. Sackler Wing of Galleries
Royal Academy of Arts, London
5 March – 30 May 2005

The Metropolitan Museum of Art, New York
23 June – 25 September 2005

Sponsored by

FARROW&BALL®
Manufacturers of Traditional Papers and Paint

With additional support from:
AXA Investment Managers

The Royal Academy of Arts is grateful to Her
Majesty's Government for agreeing to indemnify
this exhibition under the National Heritage Act
1980, and to the Museums, Libraries and Archives
Council for its help in arranging the indemnity.

EXHIBITION CURATOR
Ann Dumas
with
Norman Rosenthal
MaryAnne Stevens
Dominique Szymusiak
Gary Tinterow

CONSULTANT TO THE EXHIBITION
Hilary Spurling

EXHIBITION ORGANISATION
Susan Thompson
with
Sunnifa Hope

PHOTOGRAPHIC AND COPYRIGHT
COORDINATION
Miranda Bennion
Andreja Brulc

CATALOGUE
Royal Academy Publications
David Breuer
Harry Burden
Claire Callow
Carola Krueger
Peter Sawbridge
Nick Tite

Copy-editor: Rosalind Neely
Design: Mark Thomson
Colour origination: DawkinsColour
Printed in Italy by Graphicom

British Library Cataloguing-in-Publication
Data

A catalogue record for this book is available
from the British Library

ISBN 1-903973-47-3 (paperback)

ISBN 1-903973-46-5 (hardback)
Distributed outside the United States and
Canada by Thames & Hudson Ltd, London
Distributed in the United States and Canada
by Harry N. Abrams, Inc., New York

EDITORIAL NOTE
Measurements are given in centimetres,
height before width.

Authorship of the catalogue entries on pages
179–91 is indicated by the following initials:

KB Kathleen Brunner
AD Ann Dumas
DS Dominique Szymusiak

ILLUSTRATIONS
Full details of the textiles illustrated in this
book can be found in A Key to the Textiles
on pages 191–3.

Contents

Foreword

Henri Matisse's collection of fabrics and costumes, packed away unseen for half a century since his death, is the core – and revelation – of this exhibition. Matisse's ancestors had been weavers for generations. Textiles were in his blood. He collected them from his beginnings as a poor art student to the last years of his life when his studio in Nice overflowed with North African hangings, embroideries and the exotic costumes that adorned his odalisques, as well as traditional French textiles. Matisse's fabric collection was an archive that he called 'my working library', and he used it to furnish, order and compose his pictures. This exhibition explores for the first time Matisse's relationship with the textiles that filled every studio in which he worked. Textiles consistently provided the inspiration for radical new departures in Matisse's art, from the audacious early still-lifes to the great paper cut-outs inspired by Kuba cloths from the Congo made at the end of the artist's long life.

We owe an enormous debt of gratitude to the Matisse family, Claude and Barbara Duthuit, Jacqueline Matisse Monnier and Paul Matisse for their constant advice, guidance and generosity throughout the course of organising the exhibition. We would like especially to thank Hilary Spurling, the acclaimed biographer of Matisse, who both proposed the idea to the Royal Academy and provided constant inspiration throughout its planning and realisation. Ann Dumas, curator of the exhibition, shaped the project, together with her colleagues at the Royal Academy of Arts: MaryAnne Stevens, Collections Secretary and Senior Curator, Norman Rosenthal, Exhibitions Secretary, and Susan Thompson, who handled the complex task of organising the loans. At The Metropolitan Museum of Art, Gary Tinterow, Engelhard Curator-in-Charge, Department of Nineteenth-century, Modern and Contemporary Art, and Rebecca Rabinow, Associate Curator in the same department, have played a vital role in bringing the exhibition together. The staff of the Musée départemental Matisse, Le Cateau-Cambrésis, have also made a significant contribution. We are especially indebted to Georges Bourgeois for his dedicated research that has salvaged the history of the textile industry in Bohain-en-Vermandois. We would also like to express our gratitude to the Archives Matisse, where Wanda de Guébriant and Georges Matisse have been exceptionally generous in sharing information and advising on the exhibition. Nick Tite and Peter Sawbridge of the Royal Academy, and the editor Rosalind Neely, have worked tirelessly on the catalogue.

The success of every exhibition is reliant on its lenders. We are enormously grateful to all the institutions and individuals who were willing to part with their treasured works. It is our hope that this exhibition will reveal a little-known but fundamental aspect of Matisse to our audience, and thus enrich our understanding of this great artist.

DOMINIQUE SZYMUSIAK
Director, Musée départemental Matisse, Le Cateau-Cambrésis

PROFESSOR PHILLIP KING CBE
President, Royal Academy of Arts, London

PHILIPPE DE MONTEBELLO
Director, The Metropolitan Museum of Art, New York

Sponsor's Preface

As Matisse's art continues to enrich the lives of so many, everyone at Farrow & Ball is honoured to be part of this stimulating exhibition, which shows his works alongside the textiles that inspired them.

Our sponsorship is both exciting and humbling. Exciting, because it is the first time we have worked with the Royal Academy, and as such it will always be particularly memorable. And humbling because it associates us in such a special way with one of the greatest artists of the twentieth century.

With our passion for colour we are delighted to be sponsoring Matisse, His Art and His Textiles: The Fabric of Dreams.

MARTIN EPHSON
Director, Farrow & Ball

Acknowledgements

The curators of the exhibition wish to acknowledge with thanks the assistance afforded by individuals and the directors and staff of lending institutions (listed on p. 210), and by the following people who have helped in the realisation of the exhibition: Alexander Apsis, Ida Balboul, Kay Bearman, Lilyane Benoist, Dana Bercea, Olivier Berggruen, Anne-Sophie Bermonville, Guy Blazy, John Bodkin, Yve-Alain Bois, Bénédicte Boissonas, Arnault Brejon de Lavergnée, Christian Briend, Claire Brown, Nicole Brunne, Wendy Bryson, Alessandra Carnielli, Cathina Charalabidis, Aileen Chuk, Emmanuel Clavé, Rosemary Crill, Martha Deese, Magali Dispan de Florian, Matthew Drutt, Judith Durrer, Gregory Eades, Jean Edmondson, John Elderfield, Christopher Eykyn, Michael Findlay, Jack Flam, Dominique Fourcade, Simonetta Fraquelli, Pierre Georgel, Hugh Gibson, Thomas Gibson, John Golding, Sue Graves, Habib Guerroumi, Margit Hahnloser, Allis Helleland, Megan Heuer, Dona Hochart, Isabel Horovitz, Lucy Hunt, Chiyo Ishikawa, Ellen Josefowitz, Dorothy Kellett, Shireen Khalil, Theresa King-Dickinson, Gary Kopp, Maria Kostakis, Albert Kostenevich, Rémi Labrusse, Sophie Leroq-Ramond, Sylvie Leroq-Ramond, Adrian Locke, Anna Maris, Georges Matisse, Pierre-Noël Matisse, Patrice Mattia, John McKanna, Christopher Meyer, Zia Mirabolbaghi, Robert Mnuchin, Jean-Paul Monery, Isabelle Monod-Fontaine, Iris Müller-Westermann, Soeur Myriam, Rebecca Noonan, Linda Parry, Amanda Paulley, Meg Perlman, Roxanne Peters, Xavier Petitcol, Céline Peyre, Tom Phillips, Robert Pincus-Witten, Lionel Pissarro, Marie-Thérèse Pulvénis-de-Séligny, Denise Reid, Jennifer Richenberg, Catherine Rickman, Mélanie Riffel, Christopher Riopelle, Claude Ritschard, Pierre Schneider, Michael Scott, Natalia Semenova, Victoria Sowerby, Roberta Stansfield, Linda Sylling, John L. Tancock, Mahrukh Tarapor, Michael Taylor, Ann Temkin, Alice Tériade, Margaret Timmers, Cecilia Treves, Gérard Turpin, Marie-France Vivier, Jennifer Wearden, Nancy Whyte, Verity Wilson, Helen Wolfe and Kazuhito Yoshii.

Material World:
Matisse, His Art and His Textiles

HILARY SPURLING

'Something beyond price'

'I am made up of everything I have seen,' Matisse said towards the end of his long life.[1] This exhibition starts from what he saw in the first quarter of that life, the twenty-one years he spent at home in French Flanders in the textile town of Bohain-en-Vermandois before he ran away to Paris to become a painter in 1891. He reached the capital knowing little of the art of the old masters (whose canvases he had barely seen), and nothing of his Impressionist contemporaries (whom he had never even heard of), but already fluent in a subtle and expressive visual language with a wholly unpainterly or apictorial vocabulary. 'You can say of any particular artist that his texture is like velvet, or satin, or taffeta,' he said, analysing his predecessors in the Louvre. 'The way they do it … you can't tell where it comes from. It's magic – it can't be taught.'[2] More than half a century afterwards visitors to Matisse's studio were astonished by the opulence and delicacy of optical effect – the sheen and fall of light, the dialogues of colour – in the paintings, drawings and the great semi-abstract stained-glass and cut-paper compositions of his last years. 'Cashmere, tarlatan, muslin, damask, lace,' wrote an interviewer in 1952. 'Matisse spends his time weaving. He is a weaver. His pencil is his shuttle, his loom the weft and warp of his canvas.'[3]

Born in the grim industrial heartland of north-eastern France, Matisse came to see his whole life as a flight from the confinement of his native North towards light and colour, or what he called the 'Revelation of the South'. He discovered his identity as a painter beneath the Mediterranean sun, and he spent the greater part of his career working in the bright clear sea-borne light of Nice. Except for visits to his parents, Matisse never voluntarily returned to the cloudy flatlands of his native region, where he said afterwards he felt as if he had passed his first two decades in prison. But the direction of his flightpath was laid down in infancy. Le Cateau-Cambrésis, where Matisse was born in 1869, made its fortune from proliferating woollen mills. St-Quentin, where he went to school, was famous for its expanding lace industry and Bohain, where he grew up, for its luxury fabrics. There were no galleries, museums or art collections on display, virtually no public statuary, not even a mural in any of these smoky towns. To a child already dreaming of escape the only available outlet for a nascent visual imagination came from the sumptuous, shining, multicoloured silks produced in weavers' cottages and workshops all over Bohain.

Matisse's ancestors had been weavers for generations. Textiles were in his blood. He could not live without them. He collected them from his beginnings as a poor art student, spending tiny sums he could not afford on frayed scraps of tapestry from Parisian junk stalls, to the last years of his life when his studio in the South became a treasure-house stocked with Persian carpets,

Arab embroideries, African wall-hangings, cushions, curtains, costumes, patterned screens and backcloths. Visitors came away dazed and disbelieving, quite often disapproving, from a workshop that looked more like something from a fairytale – oriental harem, magician's lair, enchanter's palace – than the setting for any serious productive effort. But the impression of munificence was an imaginative illusion. Matisse furnished all his homes and studios from junk shops with bits and pieces that caught his eye, battered unmatched chairs, faded hangings, threadbare carpets, 'noble rags'[4] thrown out by more pragmatic housekeepers, and destined to take on a new and less transient glory on his canvases. They became the flimsy real-life partners of a luxuriant imagination,

Fig. 1
Henri Cartier-Bresson, Henri Matisse in his studio, 1943–44.
Photograph

active participants in the creation of a luxury more precious than wealth because, as Matisse said himself, 'it's something beyond price, freely available to all,'[5] a property of the eye that looked rather than the thing it saw.

Matisse's fabric collection served him as a combined archive and tool-store all his life. He called it 'my working library',[6] taking sections of it with him whenever he switched studios between Nice and Paris, sending for others as and when he needed them, constantly replenishing the collection from oriental carpet shops and clothes stores, radically extending it at intervals in the bazaars, souks and market stalls of Algeria, Morocco and Tahiti, or at end-of-season sales of Parisian *haute couture*. He packed bits of folded stuff to accompany him on his travels, painting a length of French flower-patterned silk in his hotel room in Tangier before the First World War,[7] pinning Tahitian barkcloth and Kuba fabrics from the Congo to his wall so that he could continue working

Fig. 2
Henri Matisse, **Harmony in Red**, 1908. Oil on canvas,
180 × 220 cm. The State Hermitage Museum, St Petersburg

from them in the years when he lay bedridden in a rented villa in the South of France during the Second World War.

Matisse drew on his working library to furnish, order and, on a deep, instinctual level, to compose his paintings. Fabrics made him feel at home. Like virtually all his northern compatriots, he had an inborn appreciation of their texture and design. He understood the properties of weight and hang, he knew how to use pins and paper patterns, and he was supremely confident with scissors. In 1919 he designed a Chinese emperor's cloak capable of unfurling the full length of the stage at the Paris Opéra for Sergei Diaghilev, who arranged for him to work on it in Paul Poiret's couture studio, where Matisse fell in love at first sight with a bolt of costly red silk velvet (much to the chagrin of Diaghilev, who, with uncharacteristic thrift, had budgeted for a cheaper cotton velvet). A top Parisian costumier had estimated that the gold-embroidered cloak would take three months to make, but Matisse simply spread his breadth of velvet on Poiret's biggest cutting table, seized a pair of shears, took off his shoes and climbed onto the table to cut his design out of strips of gold stuff, assembling it by eye with a team of assistants who pinned the pieces into place as he worked, and produced the finished cloak in two days flat.[8]

Matisse never repeated this feat, but he recalled it long afterwards when he started using scissors to cut or carve his works out of pure colour. He said that scissors in his hands became a tool 'as sensitive as pencil, pen or charcoal – maybe even more sensitive'.[9] His own account of how he made the emperor's cloak closely parallels the reports of people who watched him 'drawing with scissors'[10] quarter of a century later, holding a sheet of coloured paper delicately in his left hand, winding and turning it beneath the scissor blades in his right to release a stream of shapes from which he composed his gouaches

découpées, the majestic pinned-and-pasted cut-paper masterpieces of his last decade. Matisse was proud of his performance in Poiret's workshop, summoning the same casual dexterity and panache at intervals to construct props or costumes to paint or draw: a legendary plumed hat improvised with pins and fancy trimmings in 1920, a ball gown cut and pinned together in 1935 from another seductive bolt of cloth in the particular deep blue the painter loved perhaps more than other colour.[11]

But what interested him was always the dynamics of light and colour, not the intricacies of couture cut and finish. Contemporaries who criticised him for plying his colours like a weaver, or saturating his canvases in pigment like a dye-merchant, confused means with ends. Even fellow painters were baffled to find Matisse experimenting with classic weavers' techniques like pinning tracing paper to his canvases, or trying out the same composition in different colour combinations. The first and most famous recorded instance of Matisse switching colourways was the vast Harmony in Red (fig. 2), initially commissioned as a Harmony in Blue by Sergei Shchukin in 1908. Radical transpositions of this kind continued until the late great still-lifes of the 1940s, often with the help of the painted paper patterns Matisse regularly employed to test equations of form and colour in his paintings.[12] Once he invited his friend Simon Bussy to lunch to see the latest work in progress: Interior with a Dog (1934) on a grey ground that had turned red, to Bussy's astonishment, by the time Matisse asked for a second opinion after lunch.[13] Procedures that perplexed his friends made perfect sense to Matisse, who never worried that it was beneath his dignity as a painter to subvert old weavers' tricks for his own alien purposes. They became part of the continuous exacting process of appraisal and adjustment through which he struggled all his life to subdue, stabilise and balance the forces at his

Fig. 3
Seguret and Thabut, Exposition Universelle banner, 1900.
Woven banner. Georges Bourgeois Collection

experimental laboratory. It would be beyond the scope of the present survey to attempt a comprehensive study of the role played by textiles in Matisse's development at all stages. But we hope to show him using them to stimulate and release his creative powers, in much the same way as he turned to sculpture throughout his career at moments when he found the way forward as a painter blocked. The exhibition focuses on four successive shifts or turning-points when Matisse used textiles to help him break through to a new level of pictorial reality. Its aim is to peel back the layers of his imagination by looking closely at an intrinsic element that has been previously neglected, treated cursorily as an accessory, or indiscriminately subsumed under the general heading of oriental influence.

The exhibition begins with the fabulous silks produced for the top end of the Parisian couture market by the handloom weavers of Bohain during the painter's boyhood and adolescence in the 1880s. But the core of the exhibition is Matisse's own working library – 'ma bibliothèque de travail' – of fabrics, curtains and costumes, packed away in family trunks and store-cupboards for half a century since his death. These stuffs fired and fed Matisse's visual imagination from the cradle to the grave. 'Matisse, His Art and His Textiles: The Fabric of Dreams' sets out to investigate for the first time his relationship with the materials that surrounded him from birth, that filled every studio he ever had, and that spilled out from their traditional background role to take over his canvases at key points in the evolution of twentieth-century art, when the fabrics Matisse painted became themselves the actual fabric of his painting.

'All you need is daring'
One of the more impudent exhibits on show at the great Exposition Universelle of 1900 at the Grand Palais in

disposal. 'He clashed his colours together like cymbals,' wrote the critic John Berger, when Matisse died in 1954, 'and the effect was like a lullaby'.[14]

This exhibition proposes to identify some of the ways in which Matisse's fabric collection served him as an

Paris was a silk banner, woven in Bohain-en-Vermandois, showing the conventional artist's paraphernalia – a classical bust, a lyre, a painter's palette – trampled underfoot by the gods of Olympus, who hand out laurel crowns instead to representatives of the textile industry, embodying a new century of global enterprise, discovery and technological advance. Matisse had bitter memories of this exhibition, having been forced by poverty and failure to take a low-grade job painting garlands to decorate the halls of the Grand Palais. His home town won a Grand Prix in the textile section, but the selectors rejected the canvas he himself had hoped to hang in the exhibition's prestigious display of contemporary painting.[15] *Woman Reading* (1895; fig. 4) is a small, dark, forceful still-life into which the painter, by his own account, inserted a human figure in a black dress with her back turned. Its beautifully modulated halftones and sombre palette of earth colours represent the lowest category of the strict pictorial hierarchy in which a professional artist was required by the Beaux-Arts system to demonstrate proficiency before graduating to anything more demanding.

The two symbolic images – still-life and silk banner – embody Matisse's dual heritage at the end of the nineteenth century in his native region, where the narrow and coercive, backward-looking Beaux-Arts tradition was energetically opposed by local designers and entrepreneurs in charge of a confident, rapidly expanding textile industry. 'All you need is daring' was the motto of the textile trade in Bohain.[16] Four times a year the weavers of Matisse's native region put on fantastic seasonal displays for the Paris fashion market. Spring, summer, autumn and winter pattern books were composed from an exuberant profusion of silk swatches. The son and grandson of weavers, Matisse's father acquired his business training in the textile departments

Fig. 4
Henri Matisse, **Woman Reading**, 1895.
Oil on wooden panel, 61.5 × 48 cm.
Musée National d'Art Moderne, Centre Georges Pompidou, Paris

of two leading Parisian stores, and used it to open a seed-store-cum-hardware-shop with his wife, who had her own counter for selecting and preparing coloured pigments. Their eldest son, born in Le Cateau-Cambrésis in a house where previous generations of Matisses had earned their living at the loom, grew up in Bohain on a block surrounded by weavers', embroiderers' and designers' workshops among people endlessly preoccupied with finding fresh ways of combining and exploiting colour.

'It's an education without equal,' wrote a contemporary describing the constant buzz of ideas as highly competitive weavers crowded into one another's houses on their day off to inspect and analyse any ambitious new *montage* set up on the loom: 'A child who hears talk of nothing but coloured threads and looms grows attentive, knowledgeable, adroit. Daily conversation, even on a Sunday, revolves round the same subject.'[17] Throughout Matisse's boyhood and youth, the weavers of his home town prided themselves on outstripping all rivals at modernity's cutting edge. 'Picardy, thanks to Bohain, is the initiator of everything that is new in the whole of France, and indeed the rest of the world,' wrote a government inspector discussing textile design in 1897. 'Its production justifies the claim of novelty by prodigious variety, inexhaustible originality and constant innovation.'[18] Contemporary accounts agree on the delicacy and richness of the Bohain weavers' colours, their unerring sense of design and their insatiable appetite for experiment.

Their open-mindedness contrasted sharply with the academic approach that drove Matisse to despair at art school. Beaux-Arts regulations were rigidly enforced both in his school art lessons and at the morning and evening

Fig. 5
Weaver at his loom, c. 1940s.
Photograph

classes that he attended at the Ecole Quentin de La Tour in St-Quentin after he left school. Founded in the eighteenth century by Quentin de La Tour as a design school for poor weavers, it had become by the time Matisse got there primarily a provincial outpost or feeder for the Ecole des Beaux-Arts in Paris. Pupils spent years learning to copy reproductions with mechanical exactitude. 'Drawing was taught, like a dead language, as a series of prescribed routines based on plaster models of abbreviated or abridged Greek and Latin originals.'[19] The use of colour was forbidden. So was painting out of doors, or working from a live model. The aim was perfection in the copyist's art, licked clean of any trace of individual character or feeling. The split between a moribund Renaissance tradition of oil-painting and the applied or decorative arts was at its fiercest in St-Quentin, where the local art establishment fought a running battle against the freebooters of the textile industry, who wanted to modernise the curriculum and open it up to outside influences.

Individuality was highly prized – 'each shuttle … functions like a paintbrush which the weaver guides at will, and almost as freely as the artist himself'[20] – in St-Quentin's textile factories, and even more so in Bohain, where the workforce still consisted largely of pre-industrial handloom weavers, each working on his own account, taking a fierce aesthetic satisfaction in producing one-off luxury fabrics with a boldness and fluidity beyond the scope of the mass-produced and mechanised articles manufactured elsewhere in the region. Outside their own speciality these men were largely uneducated, often illiterate, but during the high-fashion textile boom of the 1880s and '90s – 'a time that saw a veritable firework display of creativity and invention'[21] – they developed a visual sophistication acknowledged as unequalled by their peers. Like the rest

of his Bohain generation, Matisse was exposed from
birth to the radical, libertarian and iconoclastic approach
of the local weavers, as well as to their disciplines of
unremitting application and exactitude. Long before he
finally reached the Ecole des Beaux-Arts in Paris (where
he repeatedly failed the entrance examination), Matisse
had absorbed the independent ethos of the alternative
decorative tradition. 'I feel like someone who arrives in a
country where they speak a different language,' he said,[22]
describing his fellow art students whose mechanised
procedures seemed to him more like a production line
than the creative autonomy he had seen at work in his
home town.

His instinctive defence as a student against the
sterility of the Beaux-Arts system was to surround
himself with the liberating colour and texture of fabrics.
'I built up my own little museum of swatches.'[23] In Paris
in the Louvre, under the direction of the generous and
perceptive Symbolist painter Gustave Moreau, Matisse
embarked on the dialogue with other painters that
sustained him intermittently all his life. He began his
formal Beaux-Arts training at Moreau's suggestion with
a study of *La Desserte* by the seventeenth-century still-life
painter Jan Davidsz. de Heem: a demonstration piece
constructed round a cascade of rumpled white napery
to show the young artist's triumphant mastery of the
techniques of his native northern school. Matisse was
always grateful to his Beaux-Arts professor for opening
doors for him in the Louvre, but Moreau, who regarded
the work of his Impressionist contemporaries as
pernicious and corrupt, was scandalised to find his star
student eventually succumbing to the influence of
Claude Monet. Pupil and teacher parted company when
another *Desserte*, Matisse's final graduation canvas of
1896–97, became the battlefield on which he grappled
with Impressionism. Over the next decade the tablecloths

Fig. 6
Henri Matisse, **La Desserte (after Jan Davidsz. de Heem)**, 1893.
Oil on canvas, 72 × 100 cm. Musée Matisse, Nice-Cimiez

Fig. 7
Henri Matisse, **La Desserte**, 1896–97. Oil on canvas,
100 × 131 cm. *Private collection. Formerly Ambroise Vollard*

Fig. 8
Henri Matisse, **Girl Reading**, 1905–06.
Oil on canvas, 72.7 × 59.4 cm. Private collection, New York

the colour conflagration that looked to Matisse's contemporaries like the work of a wild beast or Fauve.

Throughout his career textiles remained a practical, as well as an imaginative, resource on the simplest and most basic level. All his life in studios at home or on his travels in hotels and rented rooms, Matisse restarted his engine as a painter by setting out a still-life on a length of fabric, ranging from the strip of green velvet on top of the cupboard in the Woman Reading of 1895 (fig. 4), or the various scraps of folded cloth that went with him in his baggage on painting trips to Morocco in 1912 and 1913, to the extensive fabric library that supplied basic construction units for innumerable canvases between the two world wars. Textiles were humble, adaptable, unpretentious, as far removed as it was possible to get from 'le sujet noble', the noble subjects prescribed by the Beaux-Arts in Matisse's youth that implanted in him a lifelong horror of visual cliché. 'In everything he paints it's the stirrings of life itself Matisse tries to capture and transmit through his painting,' wrote an interviewer to whom Matisse in his seventies expounded a philosophy that would have been familiar to the humble weavers who raided newspapers for inspiration, pinning illustrations of the latest scientific inventions or ethnographical finds into their pattern books, treating the contemporary world as the great external repository described by Delacroix or Proust – 'in consulting it, the artist finds himself suddenly in the presence of an object that releases visions of things seen, stored and felt'.[24]

Innovation for Matisse was inextricably bound up with a decorative ornamental tradition that drew the scorn of more conventional practitioners, who regularly dismissed his colour-saturated canvases as the work of a teinturier or dye-merchant.[25] Weaving in his northern region, even at the height of its success, was beyond the scope of civilised attention. The trade flourished up to

on which Matisse set out his still-lifes steadily engulfed their traditional complement of glass, china, cutlery, flowers and fruit. In the rich glowing contrapuntal compositions painted in Toulouse in 1899, individual oranges, plates or pots lose their separate identities in an overall decorative pattern. With the explosive canvases of the Fauve period the painted stuff itself – a table-cover, the fabric of a kimono, a flowered and feathered hat – reaches out to impose its coloured rhythms over the entire surface of the canvas. In Still-life with Blue Tablecloth (cat. 7) or Girl Reading (both 1905–06) the sedate white cloth, included as a test of old-fashioned painterly skills in any trainee painter's standard repertoire, sparks off

1914, losing momentum after the First World War and collapsing altogether in the 1950s, when the weavers of Picardy and Flanders closed their workshops, destroyed their archives, sold or burned their looms, and surrendered to the 'Picard syndrome of cultural amnesia' that has since largely obliterated them and their work.[26] The anonymous weavers of Bohain left nothing but a few pattern books forgotten in attics for a century or more, and a ghostly legacy hovering in the background of the canvases of the town's most famous son, whose painting bears the same relationship to the textiles of his youth as the music of Maurice Ravel to the church-bells in the village of Ciboure, where he was born. 'It's not Ravel,' said Matisse, listening to the bells of Ciboure in 1940, 'but it's what he heard more than anything else, and knew how to convert to his use in his own way.'[27]

'A balance of forces'

Matisse converted textiles to his use in very different ways at different stages, recruiting them initially as subversive agents in the campaign to liberate painting from a tyrannical and decadent classicism that preoccupied his generation in the decade before the First World War. Flowered, dotted, striped or plain, billowing across the canvas or pinned flat to the picture plane, textiles became in his hands an increasingly disruptive force used to destabilise the laws of three-dimensional illusion. Key acquisitions in these years included a piece of *toile de Jouy*[28] (p. 80) spotted in a second-hand clothes shop from the top of a Parisian bus around 1903: a length of white fabric with a pattern of dark-blue arabesques and flower-baskets that drove or beckoned Matisse towards some of the greatest risks he ever took.[29] In 1906 he added a group of red, yellow and black prayer-mats, picked up on a journey to Algeria that became, in the words of the Russian curator Albert Kostenevich, 'a kind of voyage of

discovery to the sources of painterly language'.[30]

The boldly patterned Algerian rug hanging on Matisse's wall thrusts forward in *Still-life with a Red Rug* (1906; fig. 9) to abolish the distinction between background and foreground. In such works as the Pushkin Museum's *Still-life with Blue Pot* (1906), or the Hermitage's *Still-life with Blue Tablecloth* (1905–06; cat. 7), the rug disintegrates almost completely, dissolving into the fabric of the painting, leaving only spectral traces of its presence in a vibrant, flickering punctuation of coloured dashes, dots and commas. The cooler *toile de Jouy*, making its first appearance around 1903–04 in such paintings as *The Guitarist* (cat. 6) or *Pierre Matisse with Bidouille* (cat. 5), starts out as a relatively straightforward wall- or table-cover, but in *Still-life with Blue Tablecloth* it, too, begins to stir and swell, shooting out jagged streaks of blue to disrupt form, override perspective and divorce shape from colour. The same backcloth extends its curving lines to the human subject in *Portrait of Greta*

Fig. 9
Henri Matisse, **Still-life with a Red Rug**, 1906. Oil on canvas, 89 × 116.5 cm. Musée des Beaux-Arts, Grenoble, Agutte-Sembat Bequest

Moll of 1908 (cat. 10), where 'colour has been simplified, detail suppressed and design flattened so that the coarse features and massive forearms of the model rhyme with the blown-up arabesques of the *toile de Jouy*.'[31] In *Harmony in Red* (fig. 2), the cloth subsumes the figure, reducing the woman laying the table, along with the artificial flower-baskets and actual fruit-stands, to incidents in a pictorial pattern articulated by plunging blue arabesques that seemed to the painting's original owner[32] to career off the edges of the canvas into space.

Matisse repeatedly constructs his canvases according to the same principle at this point. It is as if the piece of cloth, carpet, screen or curtain extended its own structural rules to all the components – animate or inanimate – of any given picture, imparting control and movement, eliminating extraneous elements and intensifying others in a synthesis of line and colour that deceives the expectations of the eye, diverting it from the platitudes of appearance to the fluid, surprising, perpetually animated patterns of perception. 'It's not a different painting,' Matisse explained, when asked why he repainted the colour field of *Harmony in Red*. 'I am seeking forces, and a balance of forces.'[33] Any detailed attempt to plot the route taken by the *toile de Jouy* would show it constantly intersecting with, feeding into and reinforcing the central flow of Matisse's advance in these years. In the wildest of all its manifestations, a second *Still-life with Blue Tablecloth* of 1909 (cat. 9), the curving blue garlands dive and lunge like dolphins round a vestigial still-life. Coffee-pot, decanter and fruit-dish, each standing precariously upright on the heaving surface of the canvas, seem about to tilt and slide into the violent rhythms of the *Dance* of 1910. Matisse said he was preoccupied at the time by the intensity of colour in the *Dance*, envisaging separate areas of blue and green as flat pieces of coloured stuff, and realising only afterwards

how he had instinctively varied the pressure of his brush and the thickness of his paint 'so that the white of the canvas shone through more or less transparently, giving the impression of a rather expensive moiré silk'.[34]

Critics and public found these developments incomprehensible and almost as menacing as the parallel explorations of the Cubists. It was no accident that the one person who had virtually no problem following Matisse's new visual language as it evolved was the great Muscovite collector, Sergei Shchukin, himself the head of one of Russia's largest textile empires. Shchukin bought almost all Matisse's most radical experimental canvases between the years 1906 and 1914. Many of them – far more than scholars have suspected up until now – were painted expressly for him.[35] Unlike the Parisian art world, Shchukin was already thoroughly at home with the syntax and vocabulary of decoration familiar to Matisse from childhood, enriched and complicated in these years by successive encounters with oriental art in Algeria, Spain and Morocco, at the ground-breaking Islamic exhibition in Munich in 1910, and on a visit to Moscow as Shchukin's guest in 1911.

Born and brought up like Matisse in a world of textiles, Shchukin possessed a highly trained eye uncontaminated by academic prejudice or preconceptions. He devoted more than half his life exclusively to the family trading company of I.V. Shchukin & Sons, buying and supplying cotton goods, building up a design department that specialised in luscious colour and proliferating pattern (incorporating the latest European trends into a constantly changing repertoire of Russian folk motifs and oriental shawls with richly ornamental borders), establishing predominance in an expanding market that stretched throughout Russia, Asia and the Caucasus to Persia and India.[36] Shchukin was over forty before he began to look at paintings, and to embark on the remarkable self-education that enabled him to assemble at phenomenal speed a modern-art collection without parallel anywhere in the world before the First World War. His annual schedule was organised in these years around regular buying trips to the great oriental textile fair at Nizhny-Novgorod, and the autumn and spring salons in Paris, where the only artist whose studio he visited was Matisse.

After a patch of turbulence caused by the public uproar surrounding Shchukin's first and most ambitious decorative commissions, *Dance* and *Music*, in the autumn of 1910, the two men collaborated together in a steadily evolving partnership that had no equivalent before or afterwards for either painter or collector. Matisse started work on a major series of commissions in Seville in the winter of 1910–11, constructing a pair of riotous still-lifes around a batch of newly acquired Spanish shawls, and a blue-and-cream-coloured coverlet with a design of pomegranates that had arrested his attention in Madrid. 'Very pretty,' he told his wife, 'not in a good state, but I reckon I'll be able to work quite a bit with it.'[37] He put it at the centre of one of two canvases painted for Shchukin on his return to Paris, *The Pink Studio* (1911; cat. 12), which incorporates everything within the artist's field of vision – pictures, sculpture, fabrics, stools and model stands, the rug on the floor, the garden foliage framed by the window and the white walls washed pink by pale spring sunshine – into an inner, immaterial, coloured space of sharp greens, pinks and ochres aligned around the dark-blue quilt. A Persian rug performs a similar function in *The Painter's Family* (1911; fig. 11). In *Corner of the Artist's Studio* (1912; cat. 14), the canvas itself is made up of textiles stirring in a gust of air that lifts the striped deckchair seat and whisks round the Spanish quilt whose pomegranates have turned pink, echoing the printed flowers on the cloth screen and complementing the real leaves on black

Fig. 10
Printed cotton fabric of the type supplied by I. V. Shchukin & Sons, c. 1890s

Fig. 11
Henri Matisse, **The Painter's Family**, 1911. Oil on canvas, 143 × 194 cm. The State Hermitage Museum, St Petersburg

stems extending the drapery's folds in the watery green depths of a glazed pot. All three canvases belong to a long series in which Matisse painted, both literally and metaphorically, the view from his mind's eye.

Corner of the Artist's Studio was one of eleven paintings commissioned by Shchukin on Matisse's 1911 visit to Moscow.[38] The painter marked this unprecedented joint venture by putting on what amounted to a private retrospective in Shchukin's drawing-room, hanging almost two dozen of his most uncompromising recent works frame to frame, two rows deep, in a

display designed to accommodate a further row of eleven large new canvases along the top. Matisse left almost immediately to work on them in Morocco, dispatching batches at intervals over the next few years to Moscow to be integrated with the existing hang, which was only two or three canvases short of completion when Shchukin's collecting was halted by the outbreak of war in 1914.

'I did not fully know Matisse until I saw Shchukin's house,' wrote Jacob Tugendhold,[39] analysing the process whereby fabrics, fruit, flowers, objects, even people give

Fig. 12
Orlov, The 'Matisse drawing-room' in Shchukin's home, showing new paintings from Morocco hanging against the cornice in the top row, Moscow, 1913. Photograph

up their solid separate existence in these paintings, becoming dematerialised and abstracted. 'Not things, but the essence of things.'[40] Individually, each work produced a powerful effect, but their collective impact based on linear form and colour – 'pure colour divorced from subject'[41] – seemed to Tugendhold to take on a metaphysical existence closer to oriental than European concepts of decoration. Matisse had sucked the life out of his work-room so as to reconstitute it on canvas in the Pink (cat. 12) and Red Studios (fig. 13). A few months later he reversed the process, absorbing the pale-green walls, cherry-coloured carpet and ornamental ceiling of Shchukin's salon into the alternative world of his imagination. 'You cannot actually tell who is responsible for what,' wrote Tugendhold, 'whether it is the room that does things for Matisse, or Matisse for the room. You have only the overall impression that the whole ensemble – walls, carpet, ceiling, pictures – is the work of Matisse's hands.'[42] Visitors who contemplated these walls closely, standing in the doorway and screwing up their eyes according to their host's instructions, saw the colours flare and glimmer as life stirred in the invisible depths beyond the painted surface of canvases that seemed translucent from a distance, like stained glass. No one present ever forgot this extraordinary expanding exhibition on show in a Moscow drawing-room between 1911 and 1914, when Matisse initiated a new kind of dialogue between internal and external reality in the great decorative compositions that he said he could have made for no one but Shchukin.

'Decorative above all'

In 1918, when Auguste Renoir protested that Matisse's use of colour violated every sacred tenet of Impressionism, the younger artist explained that a picture was for him a painted space 'constructed from a convergence of forces

Fig. 13
Henri Matisse, **The Red Studio**, 1911. Oil on canvas, 181 × 219 cm. Museum of Modern Art, New York

that has nothing to do with the direct copying of nature'.[43] Matisse had come close to abstraction in a series of austere and sombre monumental works painted during the First World War. Now he wanted something more like Renoir's chromatic warmth and richness – 'Renoir's work saves us from the desiccating effect of pure abstraction'[44] – mediated by a wholly modern, almost cinematic sensibility. Matisse was fascinated from the start by the movement and fluidity of film, becoming a regular cinema-goer in the 1920s, visiting the studios and getting to know the personnel of Nice's infant film industry, staying up one night into the small hours to watch a camera crew at work on location under arc lights setting up and shooting a complex sequence controlled through a megaphone by an invisible director. 'This interested me greatly,' the painter told his wife.[45]

Matisse was himself exploring new frontiers between reality and illusion at this point in a workspace very different from any of his previous studios. After four years of living and working provisionally in modest seafront hotels, he rented a two-room apartment in Nice in the autumn of 1921, and rapidly transformed it into an environment that could be manipulated at will like a film or stage-set through the use of costumes, curtains and backcloths. He hired a local carpenter to make him a folding screen out of an Arab portière or door-curtain printed with round-headed latticed arches, and improvised another from an oriental window grille framed in eight metres of cotton cloth that he had bought and dyed himself.[46] Drapery, rugs, hangings, even the landlady's elaborate old-fashioned wallpaper began to bulge and stir, mixing, dissolving and re-forming on canvases that expand and contract like theatrical or cinematic space. Light is not so much reproduced as emitted or in Matisse's own word 'provoked' by these paintings, glimmering through, or bouncing off, a fabric screen, glinting in the folds of a dress or curtain, flickering between the lines of a red-and-white striped coverlet. Hinged curtain rods that swung out from the wall enabled him to condense and complicate his pictures, overlapping and juxtaposing stuffs, loading pattern upon pattern, blurring, magnifying or repeating images, switching focus, changing colour filters, creating and controlling pictorial tensions with a boldness and intricacy beyond anything even he had done before.

Matisse built up a costume wardrobe in the early 1920s more or less at random, starting with a consignment of Spanish shawls, experimenting with odds and ends collected in Morocco or from a Lebanese carpet-dealer in Paris, adding in the couture clothes made each season for his wife and daughter by Poiret's sister, the designer Germaine Bongard. He seems to have begun improvising costumes in much the same way as he constructed settings to suit the requirements of each successive picture after a fancy-dress ball hosted in 1921 by Renoir's son Jean (himself about to build a spectacular career as a film director). Matisse in a turban and striped robes was accompanied by his daughter dressed as an exotic, vaguely eastern beauty. Odalisque on a Terrace, painted the next day, shows her in costume with her regular posing partner, the model Henriette Darricarrère, who relaxed so naturally in this kind of outfit that Matisse promptly drove over to Monte Carlo to ask Sergei Diaghilev for the loan of one of Léon Bakst's costumes from the ballet Shéhérazade to use as a basic pattern for his own creations.[47] From now on his textile library expanded to include dressing-up chests filled with

Fig. 14
Henri Matisse, **Seated Odalisque with Raised Knee**, 1922.
Oil on canvas, 46.5 × 38.3 cm. Barnes Foundation, Merion, Pennsylvania

Moroccan jackets, robes, blouses, boleros, caps and scarves, from which his models (often film extras) could be kitted out in outfits distantly descended – like Bakst's ballet, and a whole series of films using Nice locations in the 1920s as a substitute for the mysterious East)[48] – from the French painterly tradition of orientalisation.

Matisse maintained that he needed a human presence to soften his daily confrontation with unprecedented, almost unendurable disciplines of form and colour in these years when textiles became for him, as the art historian Pierre Schneider pointed out, a means of simulating realism in pictures that were 'fundamentally abstract'.[49] Contemporaries drew their own conclusions from his paintings of odalisques in tulle tops, silk sashes and flimsy harem pants lounging suggestively on cushioned and carpeted divans. The process is at its most disconcerting in the series of paintings – including *Seated Odalisque with Raised Knee* (1922; fig. 14) in the Barnes Foundation, *Seated Odalisque with Raised Arms* (1923) in the National Gallery of Art in Washington DC and *Odalisque with a Tambourine* (1926) in the Museum of Modern Art, New York – modelled by Darricarrère in sculptural poses based initially on the figures on Michelangelo's Medici tombs. The preposterous artifice of the Barnes Foundation odalisque – a big-breasted, soft-bellied houri in a transparent skirt with rouged nipples and a fake tattoo on her forehead – makes it difficult even now to look closely at the rigorously observed and miraculously painted texture of her body and legs, set against pink-striped upholstery, seen through embroidered silk gauze, and outlined with flicks of turquoise green that stabilise the composition, establishing its architectural underpinning, and interacting with the turquoise turban as with the pinky mauves and purples of the floral backcloth in a pulsing framework of colour.

Critics routinely dismissed the work of this Nice period at the time and afterwards as decorative, shallow and self-indulgent. Matisse was stigmatised, especially in comparison with Picasso, as a worldly and essentially frivolous lightweight, an image that still lingers in the popular imagination half a century after his death. He was used to coming off badly in the perennial hostilities that had dogged him all his life between the noble art of painting and the humble, despised decorative arts of his native region. 'It's a bad mistake to give a pejorative sense to the word "decorative",' he replied. 'A work of art should

Fig. 15
Pablo Picasso, **Large Nude in a Red Armchair**, 1929.
Oil on canvas, 195 × 130 cm. Musée Picasso, Paris

Fig. 16
Hélène Adant, Matisse in his Vence studio with *moucharabiehs*, mid-1940s.
Photograph

and wallpaper tipsily surrounding her with their blowsy curves and floppy, red, almost hallucinogenic flower blobs. Nothing stimulated more vigorously the intuitive organic growth at the core of Matisse's work. 'It has to grow in me as a plant grows in the earth,' he said, discussing the unity of feeling in everything he did, 'even the odalisques.'[51] The difference is palpable in the pictures Picasso painted at this stage specifically to tease or goad his older rival – *Mandolin and Guitar* (1924) or *Large Nude in a Red Armchair* (1929; fig. 15) – where each overlapping strip of plain or patterned textile is hard-edged, fitted together like coloured tiles or patchwork templates according to a schematic concept, with none of the rhythmic energy Matisse gives to (and gets from) the warm, soft, sensuous fabrics that sway and settle in his paintings, holding or exhaling air almost like living entities.

'A certain colour of ideas'

In the late 1930s, after a period of satiation when, for five years, he virtually abandoned oil-painting, Matisse began moving back to simpler methods of construction, often starting with the shapes and patterns of particular garments that turn up again and again like favourite actors in his work. The great blue ball gown with white organdie ruffles made specifically to tempt him back to painting in 1935 was followed by a skinny, stripey, purple Algerian robe (p. 102), an expansive band of embroidered Romanian blouses, and six couture dresses picked up in 1938 at an end-of-season sale in the garment district round the rue de Boétie.[52] These dresses included the puff-sleeved, tight-waisted, diamond-patterned taffeta dance frock (p. 107) that had already won a *Grand Prix d'Elégance* in Paris, and would go on to launch an even more successful second career on Matisse's canvases. When he moved at the end of 1939 into a spacious new

be decorative above all.'[50] He saw the paintings of this period as a series of encounters in which he tested colour to the limit, constantly shifting the borders of perception in a process that culminates in the astonishing *Decorative Figure on an Ornamental Ground* (1926; cat. 26), where the seated nude seems not so much human as totemic, hard and unyielding as if carved out of wood or stone. It is the textiles that appear to surge and swell from the white wrap billowing between her thighs to the patterned rug apartment adapted to his own design at Cimiez on the heights above Nice, he set aside a whole room – *la pièce à chiffons*[53] – to house the costumes and hangings that made up his working library. Throughout the ordeals of the next few years, Matisse's portable and durable couture dresses became a kind of travelling workshop, the practical nucleus of an impromptu studio capable of withstanding all but the harshest wartime imperatives of flight, privation and disruption.

As Matisse approached his final decade, he said that, on the one hand, he had gone as far as he could in painting and that, on the other, he was coming to grips with his work as never before. 'I've been grappling for a long time with a certain colour of ideas,' he wrote in 1942, explaining that this new departure meant suppressing subtlety and refinement in the interests of letting in light and air.[54] What he lost in sensuality and opulence, he gained in clarity, intensity and power. From now on he planned to concentrate (as he had done more than thirty years before with *Dance* and *Music*) on expanses of flat, undifferentiated colour using the interchangeable media of gouache, watercolour, ultimately paper cut-outs and stained glass. Textiles remained a potent presence. He hung Tahitian pareos on his bedroom walls at Cimiez to study when he was too ill to move, and transformed his rented accommodation as an evacuee in Vence with pierced fretwork screens made from oriental textiles or *moucharabiehs* to filter light. The faithful *toile de Jouy* remained an inseparable companion to the end. But, in 1943, as he approached the last great transition in his work, Matisse replaced the paintings on his studio walls with a group of textiles very different from anything he had worked with up until then.

These were Kuba fabrics from the Congo (pp. 157–9), supple lengths of stuff with a silky pile, woven from un-dyed raffia in black, brown and rust-coloured blocks,

lines and diamonds on a paler ground. Matisse called them his 'African velvets', and coupled them with a large and richly patterned barkcloth or *tapa* from Tahiti. What he wanted from this display was the kind of imaginative jolt that had galvanised him nearly forty years before when he showed his first African wood-carving to Picasso. 'I'm astonished to realise that, although I've seen them often enough, they've never interested me before as they do today,' he wrote of the African velvets on his

Fig. 17
Matisse's studio at the Villa Le Rêve, Vence, c. 1947.
Photograph

studio walls in the summer of 1943. 'I never tire of looking at them for long periods at a time, even the simplest of them, and waiting for something to come to me from the mystery of their instinctive geometry.... I can't wait to see what [the *tapa*] will reveal to me – for it is perfection.'[55]

Matisse cut out the first of his designs in 1943 for what eventually became the album *Jazz*. Shortly afterwards he began covering his walls with small, irregular shapes cut out of coloured paper and pasted on plain paper squares or rectangles arranged, like his African velvets, in brilliant, fluid, constantly shifting combinations. One of the first of his large-scale paper cut-outs took its name – *Les Velours* (*The Velvets*) of 1947 (fig. 27) – as well as its structural alignment, from the same source. In the closing decade of his life he used the basic technique of cut, pinned and pasted paper to design anything from illustrated books, tapestry and decorative tiling to the chasubles and stained-glass windows of the chapel at Vence. Technique and content were reduced to a minimum in works of majestic simplicity and grandeur in their own right. The old seductive repertoire of

painterly skills was discarded altogether. This was a new synthesis of colour, line and movement achieved by phenomenal coordination of hand and eye – 'colours can't go wrong … unless you try to force them'[56] – through scissors as sensitive as pens or pencils. It was the ultimate expression of the alternative decorative tradition that had opened paths into unknown territory all his life.

Matisse, whose entire career came to look to him in retrospect like a flight from the sombre restrictions of his youth, recognised that he had finally returned to the vision of radiant liberated colour first glimpsed as a child in the textile towns of his native North. 'Even if I could have done, when I was young, what I'm doing now – and it is what I dreamed of then – I wouldn't have dared.'[57] He was at last composing directly in the pure colour that for him fused feeling with ideas in their deepest and most intense form. 'Painting seems to be finished for me now.... I'm for decoration. There I give everything I can – I put into it all the acquisitions of my life. In pictures, I can only go back over the same ground … but in design and decoration, I have the mastery, I'm sure of it.'[58]

I am grateful to Matisse's heirs – Claude Duthuit, Gérard Matisse, Jacqueline, Paul and Peter Matisse – for allowing me unrestricted access to family correspondence quoted here; and also to Sergei Shchukin's biographer, Natalia Semenova, who went to great pains to explore Shchukin's textile background for me.

1   Matisse, Couturier and Rayssiguier 1993, p. 361.
2   Courthion A, p. 18.
3   Verdet 1952, p. 48.
4   Letter between Henri Matisse and P. Rosenberg, 7 February 1940, Morgan Library, New York.
5   Aragon 1972, vol. 1, p. 240, note 1.
6   Letter between Henri Matisse and Marguerite Duthuit, 29 November 1943, Matisse Archives, Paris.
7   This piece of silk, which formed the basis for Basket of Oranges (1912), still exists in the Matisse family collections, and so does the blue-and-white patterned fabric in Calla Lilies, Irises and Mimosa (1913).
8   Courthion A, pp. 86–7, and see Spurling 2005, Chapter 7.
9   Verdet 1952.
10 Verdet 1952.
11 Information from the late Lydia Delectorskaya, who made and modelled the dress to Matisse's directions.
12 Matisse's use of paper patterns in the Pink Nude is well documented, but he was already employing them as early as 1912 with Periwinkles/Moroccan Garden (letter between Henri Matisse and Amélie Matisse, 31 March 1912, Matisse Archives, Paris), and continued to reshape designs with paper cut-outs as late as the Still-life with Shell of 1940 (Delectorskaya 1996, p. 122). In 1942 he transposed his green marble studio table to red as a still-life ground (letter between Henri Matisse and Pierre Matisse, 7 June 1942, Pierre Matisse papers, Morgan Library, New York), and repainted the floor of the Woman in Interior owned by Somerset Maugham three times before finally settling for pale yellow (memo between Monroe Wheeler and Alfred Barr, 19 February 1951, Barr papers, Museum of Modern Art, New York).
13 Letters between Henri Matisse and Pierre Matisse, 28 March 1934 and 7 May 1934, Pierre Matisse papers, Morgan Library, New York.
14 In the New Statesman, 13 November 1954.
15 For Matisse's connection with this exhibition, see Spurling 1998, pp. 202–3, and note 54, p. 447.
16 Eugène Plouchard, 'Le Département de l'Aisne à l'Exposition Universelle de 1900', Journal de St-Quentin, supplement, 1901, p. 143.
17 Eugène Plouchard, 'Le Département de l'Aisne à l'Exposition Universelle de 1900', Journal de St-Quentin, supplement, 1901, p. 151.
18 Marius Vachon, Les Industries d'art: les écoles et les musées d'art industriel en France, Nancy, 1897, p. 312. For Bohain's supremacy in the field of haute nouveauté, see also François Calame, 'Cachemire et betterave. La "Haute fantaisie" en Saint-Quentinois' in Tisserands de légende, François Calame (ed.), exh. cat., Abbaye de Royallieu, Compiègne, 1993, pp. 19–21, and Spurling 1998, pp. 25–7.
19 Spurling 1998, p. 35. For a detailed account of Matisse's art training at the Lycée Henri Martin and the Ecole Delatour, see Spurling 1998, pp. 36–8, 49–59, and Chapter 2, passim.
20 Eugène Plouchard, 'Le Département de l'Aisne à l'Exposition Universelle de 1900', Journal de St-Quentin, supplement, 1901, p. 154.
21 Tisserands de légende, François Calame (ed.), exh. cat., Abbaye de Royallieu, Compiègne, 1993, p. 19.
22 Matisse, Couturier and Rayssiguier 1993, p. 152, and see Courthion A, p. 20.
23 Courthion A, p. 58.
24 Courthion B.
25 For instance, Eugène Carrière in 1900, quoted in Courthion A, and André Derain in the 1930s, mentioned in Lévy 1976, p. 75.
26 Tisserands de légende, François Calame (ed.), exh. cat., Abbaye de Royallieu, Compiègne, 1993, p. 21. The Bibliothèque Municipale Guy-de-Maupassant of St-Quentin (Fonds Philippe Delaplace) has recently built up impressive regional holdings, but the widespread eradication of both artefacts and records (which continues to this day) would have made it impossible to reconstruct the Bohain weavers' achievements without the systematic campaign of research and retrieval mounted over the last ten years by Georges Bourgeois of Bohain, to whom both this essay and the exhibition owe a great debt.
27 Letter between Henri Matisse and Pierre Matisse, n.d. [probably 6 June 1940], Pierre Matisse papers, Morgan Library, New York.
28 This famous piece of stuff, which Matisse kept for fifty years and worked with more than any other, was not strictly speaking toile de Jouy. See 'A Balance of Forces' by Ann Dumas.
29 For the toile de Jouy, see Spurling 1998, pp. 364–6.
30 Copenhagen 1999, p. 203.
31 Spurling 1998, p. 411, and see pp. 416–17.
32 Sergei Shchukin.
33 Fourcade 1972, p. 129, note 96.
34 Fourcade 1972, p. 149, trans. by Jack Flam in Flam 1995, p. 118.
35 See Spurling 2005, Chapters 4 and 5.
36 Accounts of I.V. Shchukin & Sons and their range of textiles from Ivanovo. Printed Textiles 18th to Early 20th Centuries, Leningrad, 1983, and Russkaia Khudozestvennaia kultura kontza 19 – nachala 20 veka, 4 vols, Moscow, 1968–80, vol. 2 by N.V. Romanova, pp. 358–62, and vol. 4 by T.S. Gurieva, pp. 432–44. See also Kostenevich and Semenova 1993, pp. 8–9, p. 11, note 15, and p. 127, note 21 (I am assured by Natalia Semenova that the fabric samples mentioned here cannot be located in Moscow), and Semenova 2004.
37 Letter between Henri Matisse and Amélie Matisse, n.d., Sunday evening [probably 11 December 1910], Matisse Archives, Paris. The coverlet was a wedding bedspread made a century before in the Sierra Nevada.
38 Letters between Henri Matisse and Amélie Matisse, n.d. [probably 25 and 31 October 1911]. For a fuller account of this previously unknown transaction, see Spurling 2005, Chapters 4 and 5.
39, 40, 41 and 42 Jacob Tugendhold, 'Frantsuzkoie sobranie S.I. Shchukina', Apollon, nos 1–2, Moscow, 1914, pp. 22–8, trans. by Hilary Spurling. See also Semenova 2004, pp. 22–3.
43 Courthion A, p. 71.
44 Matisse quoted in Oslo 1918.
45 Letter between Henri Matisse and Amélie Matisse, n.d. [autumn 1921 or 1923], Matisse Archives, Paris. See also Dominique Fourcade, 'An Uninterrupted Story' in Washington DC 1986 for a detailed exploration of cinematic metaphors in Matisse's work.
46 Letters between Henri Matisse and Amélie Matisse, 31 August 1921 and 5 September 1921, Matisse Archives, Paris.
47 For a fuller account of this episode (documented in Matisse's correspondence with his wife, Matisse Archives, Paris), see Spurling 2005, Chapter 7.
48 For example, Rex Ingram's Garden of Allah (1926) and Alexander Wolkoff's Scheherazade (1928).
49 Schneider 1984, p. 513. See also letter between Henri Matisse and Pierre Matisse, 1 September 1940, Pierre Matisse papers, Morgan Library, New York.
50 Fourcade 1972, p. 308.
51 Matisse, Couturier and Rayssiguier 1993, p. 383.
52 Information about these dresses (to which Matisse later added another three or four) came from Lydia Delectorskaya. See also Delectorskaya 1996, pp. 232–8 et passim.
53 Jacques-Marie 1993, p. 26.
54 Fourcade 1972, p. 191.
55 Letter between Henri Matisse and Marguerite Duthuit, 30 July 1943, Matisse Archives, Paris.
56 Letter between Henri Matisse and Marguerite Duthuit, 28 September 1943, Matisse Archives, Paris.
57 Matisse, Couturier and Rayssiguier 1993, p. 128.
58 Letter between Henri Matisse and Marguerite Duthuit, 11 February 1945, Matisse Archives, Paris.

Matisse and the Metaphysics of Decoration

JACK FLAM

'I do not paint things, I paint only the differences between things,' Matisse to Louis Aragon, 1942[1]

The interaction between various levels of materiality in Matisse's painting is one of the most salient features of his art, and the way in which he orchestrated such effects is the closest thing to a 'method' that can be identified in his works. This transformative drive is apparent in all the media in which he worked – in his drawings and sculptures, as well as his paintings – and seems to be the most persistent principle behind his art. So strong is this drive that it often seems to be a determinant, rather than a by-product, of his formal concerns: a number of his pictorial strategies, from lack of finish to precariously balanced compositional structures, grew out of his lifelong engagement with the way things in the world interacted with each other conceptually, spiritually and physically.

Decorative motifs played an important role in Matisse's strategy for articulating these feelings. They provided him with a constructive element that was pictorially flexible and could also act as a subtle, but powerful, symbolic device for expressing his vision of a world in perpetual flux. Such motifs furnished dynamic elements that could be played off against the geometrical forms of architecture and made to rhyme with figures and objects. They also allowed him to suggest the interactions between different orders of things – to extend the energy within individual things beyond their physical boundaries and to create, in effect, a kind of metaphysics of decoration.

Within this domain, the arabesques and repeated floral patterns contained in textiles and wallcoverings provided Matisse with an especially rich repertory of forms. Such modalities gave him a means of inflecting his pictures with varying rhythmic structures – and of doing so in a remarkably flexible way, as the surfaces that carried the decorative motifs could be shaped and manipulated without undermining the basic credibility of the scene depicted. Furthermore, although a piece of cloth is a real object, it also contains its own pictorial field, which can function as a kind of picture within a picture and be made to interact with the objects around it in an imaginary as well as a physical way. (Unlike wallpaper, a piece of cloth is also a pliable field that can be draped or folded, or wrapped around a human body, thus offering even richer expressive possibilities.) The decorative motifs on textiles provided Matisse with a dynamic and effective means of suggesting energy and growth, and of making the space of his painting seem to expand beyond its physical bounds.

Matisse's use of decorative motifs was embedded in his understanding of the new, non-narrative means of painting pioneered by the Post-Impressionists. Because of his longtime interest in textiles, Matisse had an acute awareness of the pictorial and symbolic implications of the way decorative motifs were employed in late nineteenth-century painting – especially by Van Gogh, Gauguin and Cézanne, who used such motifs as a way of enlarging the field of meaning in their paintings despite their eschewal of narrative subjects.

In a number of cases, Matisse adapted, or alluded to, specific decorative devices from the Post-Impressionists. A work such as *Harmony in Red* (1908; fig. 2), in which the arabesques of the tablecloth and wall embody a symbolic expression of the energy contained within the early spring landscape and the fruit and flowers on the table, owes a good deal to Van Gogh's portraits of Madame Roulin as 'La Berceuse' (fig. 18), where the floral patterning that surrounds the woman becomes a symbol of her vitality and fertility. Matisse also undoubtedly noticed the way in which Gauguin used decorative motifs to reveal imaginary spaces and psychic states. In Gauguin's pictures of sleeping children, for example, the wallpaper patterns behind the children suggest their dream state; and the decorative motifs that surround the reclining woman in such a painting as *Manao Tupapau (The Spirit of the Dead Watching)* of 1892 (fig. 19) similarly evoke the mysteries of the dream and spirit worlds.[2] Matisse also

Fig. 18
Vincent van Gogh, **Lullaby: Madame Augustine Roulin Rocking a Cradle (La Berceuse)**, 1889. Oil on canvas, 92.7 × 72.7 cm.
Museum of Fine Arts, Boston, Massachusetts, bequest of John T. Spaulding

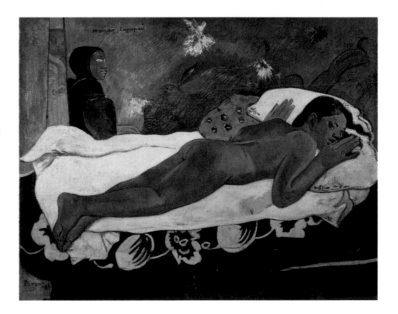

Fig. 19
Paul Gauguin, **Manao Tupapau (The Spirit of the Dead Watching)**, 1892.
Oil on burlap mounted on canvas, 73 × 92 cm. Albright Knox Art Gallery, Buffalo, New York

Fig. 20
Henri Matisse, **The Manila Shawl**, 1911. Oil on canvas, 118 × 75.5 cm.
Private collection

used patterned cloth and decorative motifs to suggest states of mind, as early as 1903, in his male and female *Guitarist* paintings (cat. 6), where the patterned fabrics that hang behind the figures seem to embody their respectively grave and highly strung states of mind (as well as the nature of the music they are playing). Similarly, the scroll-like patterning next to the woman in *Carmelina* of 1903 hints at the tensions within her, as

do the visual rhymes between the cloth and the woman's body in the 1908 *Portrait of Greta Moll* (cat. 10). In later years, Matisse put such motifs to particularly expressive use, as in his *Dream* paintings of 1935 and 1940 (cat. 51).

The bold floral patterns on the dresses of the women in Gauguin's paintings also provided a point of departure that would be echoed and elaborated by Matisse throughout his career, from *The Red Madras Hat* (1907) to the numerous late drawings and paintings of women wearing blouses and dresses decorated with elaborate floral designs. In some works, such as *The Manila Shawl* (1911; fig. 20), where the flowers emphasise the woman's breasts and pubic area, such decoration has explicitly sexual overtones. In others, such as *The Romanian Blouse* (1940), the floral designs suggest a more general sense of the woman's blossoming vitality. Photographs taken of *The Romanian Blouse* while Matisse was working on it reveal the fluid way in which he developed such metaphors, and the degree to which he conceived of different orders of things as potentially correlational.[3] At one stage, he left the woman's blouse unadorned, but painted ornate floral forms on the wall behind her. As the painting developed, the floral forms were moved from the wall back to her blouse, and as the decoration on her blouse was further elaborated, the form of her body also changed, assuming a shape that itself suggests an unfolding flower.

The musical metaphors that are sometimes evoked by Matisse's decorative motifs have similar sources. For example, his paintings of a woman seated at the piano, such as *Pianist and Checker Players* (1924; fig. 22), in which the surrounding decorative motifs evoke the music that is being played, take their inspiration from Cézanne's *Young Girl at the Piano (Overture to Tannhäuser)* (1869; fig. 21), in which the wallpaper motifs behind the piano seem to embody the music.[4]

Matisse also noticed how Cézanne frequently used

floral and leaf motifs on tablecloths, wallpaper and draperies to suggest a poetically expansive space and to create interrelations between, say, the leaf forms on a piece of fabric or wallpaper and the apples set next to them. He was alert to how Cézanne sometimes painted tablecloths or swags of cloth in such a way that the foliage and fruits depicted on them became intermingled with the real fruit lying close to them, creating an interpenetration between the imaginary pictorial world of the cloth and the tangible world of real objects.[5] Matisse frequently uses this technique – and nowhere more strikingly than in *Still-life with 'Dance'* (1909; fig. 23), in which Matisse's own painting, *Dance* (1), is placed behind a large table covered with a yellow cloth. The tablecloth is decorated with a lively pattern of floral and leaf forms, on which are set several pieces of fruit and two vases filled with flowers. Some pieces of fruit are rendered so flatly that they become conflated with the plant forms on the tablecloth, suggesting an interchange between the real fruit and the plant patterns printed on the cloth. The perspective of the picture is constructed in such a way that the forms of the table top and the mouth of the larger vase of flowers converge just at the area where one of the dancers in the painting is lunging forward, giving the impression that she is bursting out of the vase of flowers, as if to personify the energy of the forms on the table. What appears at first to be an almost random view of the artist's studio turns out to be a carefully orchestrated and symbolically charged combination of decorative, geometrical and figurative elements – full of vitality, despite the fact that literally everything depicted is inanimate.

Cézanne played an important part in Matisse's conception of the decorative – not only as a model for some of the specific pictorial tactics just mentioned, but also as a source of ideas behind Matisse's broader strategy with decoration. For, while Matisse's use of the decorative was

Fig. 21
Paul Cézanne, **Young Girl at the Piano (Overture to Tannhäuser)**, 1869. Oil on canvas, 57.5 × 92 cm. The State Hermitage Museum, St Petersburg

Fig. 22
Henri Matisse, **Pianist and Checker Players**, 1924.
Oil on canvas, 73.7 × 92.4 cm. National Gallery of Art, Washington DC.
Collection of Mr and Mrs Paul Mellon. 1985.64.25

Fig. 23
Henri Matisse, **Still-life with 'Dance'**, 1909. Oil on canvas,
89 × 116 cm. The State Hermitage Museum, St Petersburg

sometimes directly inspired by Cézanne's motifs, it was even more importantly part of his strong resistance to Cézanne – a way of escaping, or in any case deflecting, the older painter's influence. Sometimes an artist gains from an earlier artist a profound insight into reality that seems inextricably bound to a specific style, which resists further development. A great artist, however, is able to use such an insight without falling under the fatal influence of the style. Matisse related to Cézanne in this way. The decorative, in effect, allowed Matisse to explore Cézanne's view of the world with fresh eyes.

The ways in which Matisse did so are fascinating. In his Fauve paintings, he had employed bold brushstrokes set against the energised white space of the canvas ground. At that time, when he represented patterned cloth, he simply applied his brushstrokes differently in those areas, as in *Woman Beside the Sea* (1905; fig. 24), where the woman's body is differentiated from her surroundings largely in that way. The painterly practice that underlay this kind of dynamic interaction between different parts of the picture had been suggested to Matisse by the carefully modulated brushwork and the fluidity of the space in Cézanne's late works, and by the way Cézanne was able to make it seem as if the objects he painted could exist within more than one realm – and even inhabit more than one space – at the same time. In the years before the First World War, Cézanne was especially appreciated for the way in which he had been able 'to dominate universal dynamism' and reveal 'the modifications that supposedly inanimate objects impose on one another'.[6] These elements became essential to Matisse's understanding of both the world and painting.

During the course of his career, Matisse responded to these ideas in a variety of ways, and his use of decorative motifs changed accordingly. Around 1906, for example, he began to work in two distinct manners – one painterly and overtly Cézanne-like, the other relatively flat and decorative. (The two versions of *The Young Sailor* of 1906 provide an excellent example of this duality.) It was around this time that Matisse began to place emphasis on the flat patterns in textiles, rugs and wallpaper. His use of abundant, severely flattened decorative motifs gave him a means of animating the space of the 'backgrounds' in his paintings, and of creating the all-over effect of dynamism that he so admired in Cézanne, but without resorting to the passages of complexly modulated brushwork that were so typical of Cézanne's paintings.

In using decorative motifs in this way, Matisse was also able to enlarge the spatial sense of his paintings and to suggest a dimension beyond that which is literally set before our eyes. Such an expansive, overtly metaphysical vision is especially vivid in the great decorative interiors

he painted between 1909 and 1911, which display an amazing range of pictorial variety. In *Still-life with Blue Tablecloth* (1909; cat. 9), the objects seem to bob and float on the blue-and-white sea of the tablecloth, whose fictitious baskets of flowers act as a dynamic foil for the real bowl of fruit that is set next to them, and whose scroll forms are daringly made to rhyme with the shapes of the coffee pot and carafe. In the two still-lifes – *Seville Still-life* (cat. 11) and *Spanish Still-life* (fig. 36) – executed during the winter of 1910–11, the variously patterned fabrics create two rather differently voiced symphonic ensembles – each in its own way an impassioned expression of the inner energy of the explosive plants, fruits and vegetables

Fig. 24
Henri Matisse, **Woman Beside the Sea**, 1905. Oil and pencil on canvas, 35.2 × 28.2 cm. Museum of Modern Art, New York

that commingle with their intensely patterned surroundings. Once again, the feeling of animation and vitality in these paintings is so strong that it comes as something of a surprise to realise that the objects depicted in them are not only all inanimate, but also mostly inorganic.

In *The Pink Studio* (early 1911; cat. 12), the decorative motifs are handled in a more discreet, but perhaps even more imaginative way. The floral forms that climb up the cloth on the screen at the centre of the painting seem to replace the flowers that are missing from the vase placed on the stool below, and are also echoed in the branches of the real trees outside the window (an appropriate metaphor, in a depiction of an artist's studio, for creation from nothing). In *The Painter's Family* (fig. 11), completed a

Fig. 25
Henri Matisse, **Interior with Aubergines**, 1911.
Distemper on canvas, 212 × 246 cm. Musée des Beaux-Arts, Grenoble

couple of months later, the feverish decoration expresses the tensions that underlie the placid surface of the artist's domestic life.[7] And in *Interior with Aubergines* (fig. 25), painted that summer, the extravagant decorative motifs are epitomised by the floral pattern that covers, unites and fairly overwhelms the areas that are supposed to denote wall and floor, transforming the scene into an abstract meditation on a 'higher' dimension of space and time.[8]

In these works and in a number of other paintings Matisse produced between roughly 1907 and 1918, the various decorative accessories that he represented – such as rugs, tablecloths, screens, and clothing – were often radically flattened, simplified and otherwise altered. (This effect is clear if the blue cotton *toile de Jouy* Matisse owned is compared with his very different representations of it in various paintings.)[9] In this period, decorative motifs were used as overtly structural elements, rendered in a condensed sign-like way, and the compositional needs of the painting were given precedence over concerns about verisimilitude.

During Matisse's early years in Nice, he began to take a different approach to the decorative, as what he later called 'a will to rhythmic abstraction' gave way to 'corporeality and spatial depth, the richness of detail'.[10] Decorative motifs continued to play an important part in his paintings, but in another way. As Matisse's rendering of objects and the light that fell on them became increasingly naturalistic, the structural role of the decorative motifs became less apparent, even though such motifs were used more frequently. The ornamental patterns in his paintings were now often rendered in a detailed and illusionistic way, in order to enliven the rather banal settings of his subjects and to create a general ambience. They also served as a paradoxical counterbalance to the more specific, time-bound nature of Matisse's imagery at this time.

Fig. 26
Henri Matisse, **Odalisque with Magnolias**, 1923 or 1924. Oil on canvas, 65 × 81 cm. Private collection, New York

As Matisse's style changed, he became more and more interested in rendering the particularities of his subjects. Yet he knew, with over twenty years of experience, that dwelling on the particularities of things did not necessarily produce the greatest kind of art. As far back as 1908, he had written that he wanted his paintings to transcend the 'succession of moments which constitutes the superficial existence of beings and things, and which is continually modifying and transforming them' by inventing forms that would express their 'more essential character' and 'give to reality a more lasting interpretation'.[11]

Now that he was giving new emphasis to fleeting surface effects, decorative elements furnished a way of imparting greater pictorial density to his paintings. Matisse's rendering of various kinds of decorated cloth (frequently including, for the first time, translucent curtains) lent many of his pictures created during the 1920s an abstracted musical quality that allowed the

Fig. 27
Henri Matisse, **The Velvets (Les Velours)**, 1947.
Gouache on paper, cut and pasted, 51.5 × 217.5 cm.
Kunstmuseum, Basel

viewer to appreciate their pictorial richness almost despite their subjects.

For example, in a painting such as *The Moorish Screen* (1921), the profusion of decorative elements operates in a very different way from those in the 1911 *Interior with Aubergines* (fig. 25). In this work, as in so many others of the 1920s, the intense decoration creates a kind of atmospheric ambience, which is enhanced by the lightness of the brushwork and by the relative looseness of the patterns it describes. In many of Matisse's paintings during this period, a remarkable 'porosity' seems to exist between things because of the way that large areas of highly patterned surface are kept open and breathing. Unexpected pictorial contrasts are also frequently made

to carry much expressive weight. In the intensely decorated *Moorish Screen*, for example, the two women wear plain white dresses, which make them seem to absorb the intense decoration around them. In other paintings, such accents may be furnished by strategically located bursts of flowers or by the interaction between a design on a piece of cloth and a vase that is placed upon it.

Decorative motifs play an especially interesting role in Matisse's paintings of odalisques, which are often animated by some sort of floral backdrop. Paradoxically, these decorative patterns both enhance the women's sensuality and depersonalise it. In the sultry *Odalisque with Magnolias* (1923 or 1924; fig. 26), for example, where the woman's body is set against the violet floral patterning

on the screen behind her, the bursting magnolias act as a sumptuous metaphor for her sexuality. In this work and in related paintings, the intensity of the viewer's confrontation with the model and her provocative sensuality are mediated by the decorative elements, which in an odd way both enhance and generalise the erotic charge of the individual woman by insisting on the artificial and synthetic quality of the painted image. It was largely through such decorative effects that Matisse was able to realise his stated goal during his early years in Nice of balancing 'the typical and the individual at the same time, a distillation of all I see and feel in a motif'.[12]

At first glance, such paintings appear to have little to do with Cézanne, even though Matisse spoke glowingly of him during the 1920s, and stated that his 'masters' were 'Cézanne and Renoir'.[13] Yet it is apparent that Matisse was still wrestling with the lessons that he had learned from Cézanne. The influence of Cézanne is especially evident in the way in which Matisse continued to try to integrate abstract and synthetic elements with a more tangible and mimetic general ambience, and in the way he used the lively accents of decorative patterns to animate the 'background' spaces of his paintings.

During the 1930s, Matisse underwent another important shift in style, and the objects in his paintings became increasingly flattened and removed from real space. Starting in the mid-1930s, the decorative elements in his work once again became more synthetic and more sign-like – as did all of the forms in his paintings. It is perhaps not merely coincidental that in 1936, just as he was making the transition into his late style, he was willing to give up the Cézanne painting of *Three Bathers* that he had owned since 1899, and that had been a kind of talisman for almost forty years. 'It has sustained me morally in the critical moments of my venture as an artist,' he wrote when he handed it over to the Musée du Petit Palais, Paris: 'I have drawn from it my faith and my perseverance.'[14]

Around this time, which coincided with his early cut-outs, Matisse began to speak of his work in terms of the invention of what he called 'signs'. He used this term in a general, rather than in a strictly semiotic, sense – that is, what the *Random House Dictionary* calls 'a conventional mark, figure, or symbol used as an abbreviation … or to represent a complex notion', and what Matisse himself described as 'the briefest possible indication of the character of a thing. The sign'.[15] In his late paintings, Matisse was even more daring in the ways he combined objects to emphasise the affinities that underlay their apparent differences. When looking at his paintings of the late 1930s and 1940s, the viewer is simultaneously asked to accept the objects for what they are – a woman, a table, a vase of flowers, perhaps some fruit, and yards of vividly patterned cloth – and at the same time to understand that, taken together, these things also suggest another

kind of reality and signify another kind of space. This other kind of space is neither strictly two-dimensional nor fully three-dimensional, neither specifically ethereal nor corporeal. It is in effect a kind of 'third space', a new reality that is created by the differentials between what is shown and how it is represented. Within this context, decorative motifs mediate between the representation of the object as a real thing and the representation of the object as part of an ensemble of forms that exists in a world apart, and which seems to follow its own rules – rules determined in large measure by the ways in which pictorial energies are guided and modulated by the pulse of decorative patterns.

Matisse's late paintings and cut-outs marked an apogee in his use of both signs and decoration. In some of the cut-outs, the decorative structure is in effect all that remains – as an idea, an organising principle, and as an expansiveness that transcends, almost disdains, the mere physicality of things. In a number of the late cut-outs, such as *Les Velours* (1947; fig. 27), the entire work is quite literally organised in terms of the structural principles of textile decorations.

The fluid and open kind of space made possible by decorative motifs allowed Matisse to produce works that to some degree parallel the process of consciousness itself by providing a pictorial equivalent for the multiplicity and complexity of our experience of the world.

1 Louis Aragon, 'Matisse-en-France' in *Henri Matisse Dessins: thèmes et variations*, Paris, 1943, p. 37.

2 See, for example, Gauguin's *The Little Dreamer* and *Sleeping Child*, reproduced in *The Art of Paul Gauguin*, exh. cat., National Gallery of Art, Washington DC, 1988, pp. 29 and 37.

3 The photographs are reproduced in Monod-Fontaine, Baldassari and Laugier 1989, pp. 96–97.

4 Matisse was acutely aware of analogies between painting and music. In Frank Harris's account of his meeting with Matisse in 1921, he recounts how 'several times in talking he illustrated some peculiarity of painting with musical examples'. In Frank Harris, 'Henri Matisse and Renoir' in *Contemporary Portraits, Fourth Series*, London, 1924, p. 187.

5 Cézanne's *Still-life with Apples* (c. 1895–98; Rewald 804), Museum of Modern Art, New York, is an excellent example of this technique.

6 Albert Gleizes and Jean Metzinger, Du 'Cubisme', 1912; trans. Robert L. Herbert, *Modern Artists on Art: Ten Unabridged Essays*, Englewood Cliffs, 1964, p. 4.

7 On the relation between this painting and Matisse's domestic situation, see Flam 2003, pp. 78–79.

8 This effect would have been even stronger when the painting was surrounded by its original painted false frame, now lost, which contained a continuation of the floral motifs that appear inside the picture space, rendered in reversed colours and values, dark violet on light. The repeated all-over floral forms transform the painting into a decorative field similar to that found in a piece of cloth, and in a sense anticipate the structure of some of the late cut-outs.

9 Even the colour of the cloth is sometimes radically altered, as in *Harmony in Red*.

10 In a 1919 interview with Ragnar Hoppe ('På visit hos Matiss' in *Städer och Konstnärer, resebrev och essäer om Konst*, Stockholm, 1931; translated in Flam 1995, p. 76), Matisse drew a distinction between what he called 'concentration and more intense expression both in line and colour' and 'corporeality and spatial depth, the richness of detail'. Decades later, he explained this difference to André Verdet (*Entretiens, notes et écrits sur la peinture: Braque, Léger, Matisse, Picasso*, Paris, 1978, p. 124) as follows: 'A will to rhythmic abstraction was battling with my natural, innate desire for rich, warm, generous colours and forms, in which the arabesque strove to establish its supremacy.'

11 Matisse 1908, pp. 731–45; trans. in Flam 1995, p. 39.

12 Ragnar Hoppe, 'På visit hos Matiss'; trans. in Flam 1995, p. 76.

13 See Harris, 'Henri Matisse and Renoir', p. 188. Matisse spoke at length about Cézanne, whom he called 'a sort of god of painting' in a 1925 interview with Jacques Guenne; see Flam 1995, p. 80.

14 Letter to Raymond Escholier, 10 November 1936. First published in Escholier, *Henri Matisse*, Paris, 1937, pp. 17–18; trans. in Flam 1995, p. 124.

15 Aragon, 'Matisse-en-France'; trans. in Flam 1995, p. 151.

'What Remains Belongs to God': Henri Matisse, Alois Riegl and the Arts of Islam

RÉMI LABRUSSE

I

Lilah al-bāqī, 'what remains belongs to God'. The beauty of appearances has the right to be extolled – and brought into play – only to the point at which it reveals its own fragile impermanence, its ephemeral stirrings of life-force that can be bestowed and withdrawn at any moment, in contrast to baqa, the only permanent reality, the eternal and invisible base upon which the divine principle reposes.[1]

Oleg Grabar, the historian of Islamic art, suggests that the importance accorded to decorative art in Islamic culture is connected with this summarised version of Islamic thought.[2] Substantially the same formula can be detected in almost all twentieth-century attempts to understand the basic features of the Islamic aesthetic, those innumerable adornments whose fragile materials echo the lack of distinction between artist and anonymous artisan. A world of interdependent forms, dissolving brilliantly one into the other, is produced in the midst of daily life. Dominique Clévenot has called them the 'arts of the veil',[3] moving screens which stand at the exact spot where the fragile tenuity of worldly things and the dizzy designation of absence intersect: the insubstantial splendour of the veiled world beyond. In a paradoxical flash, forms are revealed thenceforward as a bonus; they create a momentary dazzle that has neither past nor future. They are rendered more playful, lighter – perhaps we should say they are redeemed – by not having to bear the weight of being: the age-old question of the connection between image and substance suddenly seems to disperse like smoke.

Not only the arabesque – a motion from within whose destiny and great strength, according to Ernst Kühnel (quoting Goethe), is to possess neither beginning nor end[4] – but also textile art itself has often been interpreted by art historians as bearing privileged witness to this vision; by means of these woven surfaces, the free forms and colours which bring instant light and life to a space when they are unfurled, and which can just as rapidly be folded and put away, be piled on top of one another, be adapted to different kinds of space, can disappear and then bloom once more.

A fabric is like a tactile, visible second skin, whose thrilling presence seems to have borrowed its sensual intensity and its subtle fragility from life itself; while the spectator's gaze wanders across its woven web, the fabric causes the object it covers to disappear. Perhaps this is the origin of the brilliant fabrics which, according to tradition, covered Mecca's holy Kaaba, the sacred stone of black basalt, regarded by Muslims as the navel of the earth, that will bear witness to humanity's sins on the Day of Judgement;[5] and the royal textile factories, the government monopolies so jealously guarded by the Abbassids in Baghdad and the Fatimids in Cairo (following Byzantine custom), that produced the most costly and highly prized gifts.[6]

2

We know that European art and art history developed a way of interpreting Islamic art through textiles, feeding a growing fascination with these products of the Muslim Middle East that began to develop in the late nineteenth century. The most important works of Islamic art, whether newly discovered or rediscovered, became the subject of research and study, and through them the non-European arts and the idea of decorative art were enthusiastically annexed to the history of art.

Prolonging a centuries-old tradition of admiration for Islamic textiles, historians made such textiles the paradigm for 'Saracenic' creative inspiration, at the same time ascribing unrivalled skill in this field to those regions in which Islamic culture flourished. For example, on the occasion of an exhibition of Islamic art (which included some exceptional Safavid carpets) at the Union Centrale des Arts Décoratifs in Paris in the summer of 1903, Gaston Migeon, the show's organiser, wrote: 'No painted work could ever achieve such accords of superlative harmony and unusual subtlety as the great

weavers of Isfahan have sometimes achieved in these admirable pieces.'[7] This love of fabrics played a leading role in the re-evaluation of the idea of decorative art, which was now beginning to be considered on its own merits rather than as a secondary area of fine art.

Between 1878, when the critic and connoisseur Henri Lavoix (a tireless champion of 'oriental' art) judged that the 'Arab' peoples, 'doggedly imprisoned in ornamentation', 'do not occupy a very important place in the history of art',[8] and 1903, when Migeon wrote of Islamic art as 'that marvellous art which, with Japanese art, is the most intoxicating in the world', embodying 'the *summum* of decorative skill, a high point which has never been surpassed, nor even approached',[9] a major revolution had taken place within which fabrics and carpets played a leading part. Everywhere (and particularly in the wake of William Morris's masterly example in England), the imitation of Muslim 'decorative artists' was encouraged; only thus would Europe be spared the collapse of any notion of aesthetic decoration in the manufacturing arts.[10] Collections – to mention only the most prestigious examples in France at the time, one in the Musée Historique des Tissus in Lyons from 1891[11] and another at the Musée des Arts Décoratifs in the Louvre from 1905[12] – began to give prominence to the Muslim East. Finally, speculation and theories about the origins of the textile arts, and the reasons why they flourished so exceptionally in the countries of the Eastern Mediterranean, began to proliferate.

3

Nowhere did the formation of collections and academic debate burgeon so intensely as in Germany and Austria at the end of the nineteenth century and the beginning of the twentieth. Although the collections in Paris and Lyons were among the largest and most comprehensive

Fig. 28
Fragment of carpet with medallions from Iran (Kerman?), seventeenth century.
Wool and silk, 515 × 457 cm. Exhibited in Paris in 1907 and in Munich in 1910,
no. 5. *Philadelphia Museum of Art, Philadelphia*

in existence,[13] those in Berlin (thanks to Friedrich Sarre
and Wilhelm von Bode), Munich and Vienna were also
of the first rank. In addition, they produced a series of
studies that can without exaggeration be hailed as a major
advance in the history of art.

It is to Alois Riegl, curator of the department of
textiles at the Osterreichisches Museum für Kunst
und Industrie in Vienna, that this advance is mainly
attributable. Riegl gave a powerful critique of the
materialist approach, which, in the wake of Gottfried
Semper, then dominated stylistic analysis. The disciples
of the great architect and theoretician explained away the
forms of the earliest ornamental patterns as the outcome
of the technical constraints of the weaving process. Riegl,
in his *Stilfragen*, reversed this, identifying the concept of

decoration as the source of textile art. By considering
'personal adornment' as 'one of man's most basic needs',[14]
he related this need to a specific psychological feature
which in 1893 he had not yet named *Kunstwollen*, simply
describing it as 'this "something" in us which makes
us take pleasure in the beauty of form, and which
champions of the technico-materialistic origins of the
arts have as much difficulty in defining as we do'.[15]

Although this reversal may have detracted
significantly from the value of the textile as such, it
nevertheless drew its initial vitality from the passionate
relationship between Riegl and oriental carpets.[16] Thus
the first important theory of decorative art as a 'superior
unity',[17] which nothing – neither technical skill, nor
history, nor geography, nor race – could explain except,
in its irreducibility, an autonomous 'will for art'
(*Kunstwollen*), was born from the extreme admiration of
an art historian for the garments, velvets and carpets of
the 'old Orient' in the reserves of his museum. This was
undoubtedly combined with his despair at the decadence
of similar products in contemporary Europe and, even
more, at the inexorable spread of deadly functionalism
to colonial outposts all over the world.[18]

It was at this period that Riegl first clearly formulated
his version of the principles of Islamic aesthetics: an
'anti-naturalistic tendency verging on abstraction';[19] and,
above all, the 'law of infinite relationships', the Arabs'
'absolutely basic law of the constitution of the arabesque
and surface decoration'[20] which, to his way of thinking,
consisted in making the relationships between forms
more important than the forms themselves. To this he
was to add some years later the idea of the art of 'the pure,
subjective surface', the apotheosis of free optical play
with lines and colours, completely at odds with the
tactile nature and mimetic preoccupations of three-
dimensional form.[21]

4

In 1910, five years after Riegl's death, an exhibition of masterpieces of 'Mohammedan' art was held in Munich. Matisse travelled that October to view the thousands of objects exhibited.

Even now this exhibition remains the most outstanding event ever devoted to Islamic art, a kind of act of allegiance to the departed creator of *Kunstwollen*. To begin with, textiles were its main focus, in quantity as well as quality (figs 28, 29).[22] Secondly, in the monumental catalogue published later by Friedrich Sarre and Fredrick Robert Martin, the analytical essays on fabrics and wooden objects were written by two of Riegl's disciples, Moriz Dreger and Ernst Kühnel respectively, and the pair left clear evidence of the formalism inherited from their mentor in their characterisations of Islamic *Kunstwollen*. Dreger, for example, reflects that textiles, in which the laws of 'infinite relationship' and of 'absolute surface' are displayed in their purest form, have the same effect on the human mind as music, creating harmonies with their linear rhythms and their colourful chords.[23] Finally, in a more general way, in the group of texts relating to the exhibition, enthusiastic appreciation of the greatness of Islamic art is often based on opinions originally developed by Riegl: praise for a society's creative skills based on domestic craftsmanship; the idea that the arabesque, the highest point of Islamic artistic invention, proceeds from an internal transformation of the Hellenistic *palmette* and *rinceau*; and, above all, the final definition of the arabesque (in the history of forms) as 'the highest expression of an abstract feeling for beauty'.[24]

5

Clearly, there is no reason to suppose that Matisse, during the week he spent in Germany visiting the Munich exhibition, was aware of such debates, even though he had acquired a copy of the pocket catalogue for his visit (Hans Purrmann, his disciple and a great admirer of Islamic art,[25] accompanied him to Munich and could have translated the catalogue for him).

However, the very fact of Matisse's visit demonstrates the way shared intuitions predisposed various artists, hungry for radical aesthetic change, and art historians from the most advanced circles towards Islamic art at this time. 'It is becoming clear', Riegl had written in 1901, 'that science itself, despite its apparent autonomy and objectivity, nevertheless finds its orientation in the

Fig. 29
Prayer rug from Turkey, sixteenth century. Wool and silk, 172 × 127 cm. Exhibited in Munich in 1910, no. 156. Kunstgewerbemuseum, Berlin

dominant tendencies of contemporary thought: neither can the art historian detach himself completely from the artistic tendencies of his contemporaries.'[26]

'For whether we want to or not, we belong to our time and we share in its opinions, its feelings, even its delusions,'[27] remarked Matisse in his 'Notes of a Painter' in December 1908. He immediately sent the text of 'Notes of a Painter' to Odilon Redon,[28] who had just received a commission to make cartoons for the Manufacture des Gobelins;[29] soon Redon was gazing with amazement at

Fig. 30
Odilon Redon, Design for a prayer rug, 1908–09.
Distemper on canvas, 92.8 × 66 cm. Musée d'Orsay, Paris

the 'shreds of fabrics from Byzantium and Persia' in the Musée des Tissus in Lyons,[30] while designing more and more prayer rugs heavily influenced by Islamic art (fig. 30).

A few years earlier, Paul Signac (whose intellectual support was so invaluable to Matisse until 1906) had written of the Neo-Impressionists' latest scientific colour theories: 'The least oriental weaver knows as much about them.'[31] In 1908, Henri-Edmond Cross, himself a Neo-Impressionist, congratulated Matisse on the nature of the 'highly ornamental tapestry' in *Harmony in Red* (fig. 2), regretting only the 'prosaic' nature of the chair 'in this beflowered ensemble with arabesques chasing each other over the whole surface'.[32]

In the wake of the Nabis, who since 1890 had been pursuing speculation about decorative art to great lengths, Maurice Denis, himself disposed in 1905 for a return to classical tradition, criticised Matisse for having out of arrogance wished to exceed 'decorative artifice, as imagined by Turkish and Persian carpet weavers' in favour of 'something even more abstract … painting removed from any contingency, painting for its own sake, the pure act of painting'.[33] In the opposite camp, the young critic Michel Puy, related to the Fauves through his brother Jean, was delighted to observe in 1910 that Matisse's paintings, 'assembled in a gallery … furnish the walls in sumptuous fashion and match the tonalities of the handsomest carpets'.[34] In short, to an entire generation, carpets and fabrics, decoration and the Orient were inextricably linked in contemporary debate; there was a renewal of painting on the horizon, and even, on a broader scale, a renewal of the way of looking at images in the West.

It is unusual to find anyone who remains unaware of the very powerful presence of this vein of inspiration in Matisse's revolutionary art, either to grieve over it – he 'confused two genres: the art of the painter and the art of the tapestry-maker', complained the critic Jean-François Scherb in 1910[35] – or to give credit to the artist – thus Louis Vauxcelles in 1906, just as he made a permanent break with Matisse, could still comment that some of his paintings possessed the 'radiance of oriental woollen fabrics'.[36]

6

'Revelation thus came to me from the Orient,' said Matisse at the end of his life, still dreaming of the Munich exhibition.[37] This revelation of the Orient came to him through fabrics, and conversely, the revelation of fabrics came to him through the Orient, both visually and conceptually.

The milieu into which it arrived immediately interpreted the Islamic references to suit its own needs, and these references continued to expand and to become more explicit as they embraced the Coptic, Sassanian and Byzantine worlds (fig. 31).[38] The exhibition of Islamic art at the Louvre in 1903 gave prominence to textiles and carpets from Parisian private collections. In February–March 1907, in the same galleries, the Union Centrale des Arts Décoratifs organised an exhibition 'of oriental velvets, carpets and silks', which was, according to Maurice Demaison, 'the most comprehensive collection ever presented to the Parisian public'.[39] Also featured were Coptic and Byzantine fabrics, Fatimid silks, Safavid embroideries and carpets, and Ottoman velvets from Bursa, among other pieces. One of the largest lenders was the Armenian dealer Dikran Kelekian,[40] whom Matisse encountered during this period, during which Kelekian's collection gained world fame for its Turkish and Persian art (in 1910 in Munich he offered to lend, among other things, one hundred examples of Bursa velvet).[41]

Fig. 31
Fragment of fabric from Byzantium (Asia Minor), sixth–eighth centuries. Silk, 240 × 140 cm. Exhibited in Munich in 1910, no. 2,252. Rijksmuseum, Amsterdam

Matisse's ability to contemplate the journey to Munich in October 1910 can only be explained by his association over the preceding years with a group of personalities who supported his efforts, sharing his predilection for the Orient as it was embodied in oriental

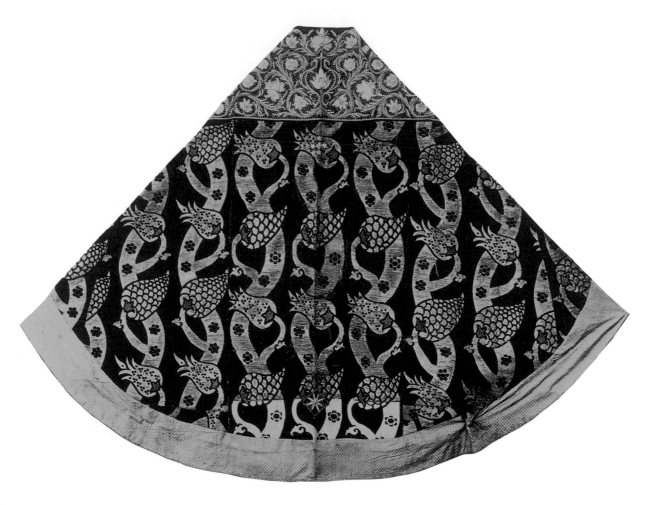

Fig. 32
Brocade tunic from Turkey or Central Asia.
Exhibited in Munich in 1910, no. 2582. Formerly in the Piotr Shchukin Collection

textiles. Among them were Gustave Fayet, who entertained Matisse in 1905 and encouraged him to make the trip to Algeria in 1906, before completing his own career as a designer of carpets;[42] the Stein family, surrounded by Turkish carpets, Chinese enamels and works of contemporary art in rue de Fleurus; Karl-Ernst Osthaus, who in 1908 invited Matisse to visit his museum in Hagen where he had some important examples of Coptic and Persian fabrics, some of which were to be lent to Munich;[43] Sergei Shchukin, who was very close to his brother Piotr, whose collection of Islamic textiles was exhibited with other masterpieces in Munich, before Matisse saw them for a second time in Moscow in 1911 (fig. 32);[44] the dealer Charles Vignier who, having converted Jacques Doucet, the celebrated couturier, to Islamic art, introduced Matisse to Doucet;[45] and Alphonse Kann, an avid collector who became a personal friend of Matisse in 1910, and in whose home, according to Pierre Loeb, 'on a background of Gothic tapestry and Coptic fragments, a Matisse rubbed shoulders with a painting from Fayoum'.[46] This was, in short, a very proactive group, busy adapting to the modern visual revolution the treasures of Islam currently being offered to discerning collectors on the European art market, a market patently enriched by colonial (or in the case of Iran and the Ottoman Empire, para-colonial) plunder.

7

In addition to Hans Purrmann and Albert Marquet, who accompanied Matisse to Munich, the painter met one of the liveliest of his 1909–14 acquaintances while he was there. The Englishman Matthew Stewart Prichard provided historical and aesthetic ammunition for the comparison between oriental art (at the centre of which he placed Byzantium) and Matisse's own pursuits. He based his ideas on a highly personal interpretation of the work of the philosopher Henri Bergson. In Prichard's opinion, the *élan vital* or 'life-force' proposed by Bergson was aroused by 'decorative' art, encouraging the onlooker to action rather than contemplation. Prichard spent most of the summer in Munich, fascinated by the great exhibition. He described it to his friend Isabella Stewart Gardner in Boston, emphasising the value of the Islamic decorative aesthetic that was so diametrically opposed to Western mimetic art: 'The error of exaggerating the importance of representation which distinguishes all European art except Byzantine was avoided in the Orient where, with a prescience of its impossibility and vulgarity, the authorities or tradition forbade its encouragement. In compensation, what carpets, what pottery, what crystals, what woodwork, what architecture, and if modern life wishes to look to private rather than to public efforts, what evidence of the unlimited exaltation of the house and palace that these relics, these 'shadows of a magnitude', provide us!'[47]

Others of Matisse's acquaintance, some of them also friends of Prichard, converged on Munich too. One of them was Thomas Whittemore, who had not yet founded the Byzantine Institute of America, but already noted admiringly, with regard to a Persian tunic with a black background (fig. 33), that it was 'done in the manner of Matisse'.[48] Also in Munich was Roger Fry, who had met Matisse in 1909 and who, a few years before he created the Omega Workshops (in which fabrics were to occupy an important position, strongly influenced by the French painter), had expressed his enthusiasm in the pages of *The Burlington Magazine* for the 'incredible beauty of Fatimite textiles' and on a more general note for 'an art in which the smallest piece of pattern-making shows a tense vitality even in its most purely geometrical manifestations'.[49]

Fig. 33
Persian tunic, sixteenth century. Wool and silk, height 112 cm. Exhibited in Munich in 1910, no. 2,369.
Osterreichisches Museum für Kunst und Industrie, Vienna

Fig. 34
Henri Matisse, **Still-life with Geraniums**, 1910. Oil on canvas, 94.5 × 116 cm.
Staatsgalerie moderner Kunst, Munich

Finally, while in Munich, Matisse met two of his German collectors, both admirers of oriental art: Hugo von Tschudi, the new director of the Bavarian museums, and his assistant Heinz Braune. Tschudi had returned from Japan in 1909 via Egypt; although already seriously ill, he was co-president of the working committee of the Islamic exhibition, and had recently added Matisse's Still-life with Geraniums (fig. 34) to his impressive collection of modern art.[50] He considered Matisse 'one of the most important painters of this century',[51] and chose this particular painting in February 1910, preferring it to a portrait because of the 'strong bold colours'[52] of its composition, at whose heart the main pattern is a width of toile de Jouy transposed – as in *Harmony in Red* (1908;

fig. 2) – in a way which owed far more to the art of Islam than to eighteenth-century France. (This may explain the enthusiasm it aroused in Kandinsky,[53] who was also engaged at this period in intense consideration of the life-giving effect that oriental decorative art was having on contemporary art.)

8

Matisse loved oriental textiles throughout his life, and possessed a collection of Islamic and Coptic pieces. If we are to believe the memoirs he dictated to Pierre Courthion, he began searching for 'Persian fabrics' in the early years of the century, only managing to resist the desire to collect them by claiming to find the same effect in the iridescent light effects of an 'evening sky'.[54] This did not prevent him giving one of these 'scraps' pride of place in the centre of his painting *The Red Studio* at the end of 1911: 'the warm blacks of the border of a piece of Persian embroidery placed above the chest of drawers', as he put it in a letter to Shchukin from Tangier in February 1912, hoping in this way to encourage his patron to accept 'the most musical of all [his] paintings'.[55]

Several photographs taken during the last years of the artist's life show an Ottoman embroidery lovingly spread over his bed-head (fig. 35), or laid beside his own flower drawings. In 1918 in Nice Matisse asked his wife to 'take care of the carpets that are in the studio'[56] (they had been brought back from Algiers in 1906, from Spain in 1911, from Morocco in the following year or simply purchased in Paris). In 1920 Marguerite Matisse informed her father that a passing visitor from Japan had admired his collection of textiles, in particular his 'Coptic embroideries'.[57]

All this is evidence of Matisse's passionate interest in oriental art which, between the two world wars, extended to *tapas* from Polynesia[58] (see p. 161) and Kuba raffia velvets from the Congo[59] (see pp. 157–59).

9

More important than the provenance or specific quality of the objects Matisse possessed is the way in which he used them. In *Spanish Still-life*, one of the two Seville still-lifes (fig. 36 and cat. 11), he deliberately transformed an antique Spanish wool carpet with blue patterns on a white ground that he had recently purchased from an antique dealer in Madrid[60] into a tiled wall. The pattern of stylised pomegranates, flowers and animals, white on a blue ground, bears a striking resemblance to Seljuk or Ottoman art (fig. 37), while also echoing the Nasrid decorations in the Alhambra (fig. 38), that 'marvel'.[61]

Conversely, in *The Red Studio* (fig. 13), an Islamic fabric is unrecognisable as such but is used purely to provide propulsion for the forms, a nucleus of coloured energy, associated with the artist's paintings and with the flowers in the vase – also Persian – in the foreground. This gives tempo to the glowing Venetian red room, as if everything had been set in motion at the same time, in unison. Unwittingly, Matisse subscribes to the theory of Islamic decoration that Riegl had developed twenty years earlier: the artistic essence of the object is not the product of its technique (a fabric can embody the same *Kunstwollen* as a tiled panel, and vice versa), nor of its iconographic content; rather, it is the product of the way the form is experienced inwardly – in compliance with the laws, in this case, of infinite relationship and absolute surface.

Matisse's use of textiles responds to these laws by putting pictorial space under tension in two ways: rhythm and folds. The rhythmical repetition of pattern is the founding principle of an abolition of boundaries, of the *Grenzenlosigkeit* which in 1910 Moriz Dreger, following Riegl, linked to the Islamic 'idea' of the textile, sustained by 'the joy of colour'.[62] A powerful passage of identical purple motifs in *Interior with Aubergines* (fig. 25) unifies the surface of the painting by superimposing

Fig. 35
Robert Capa, Henri Matisse
at the Hotel Régina, Nice,
with a nineteenth-century
Ottoman embroidery on
the wall, 1941. Photograph

itself over the complex spatial effects, projecting the chromatic vigour of the surface beyond the boundaries of the frame. As for the folds or compartments (the latter produce a similar effect) that are created by super-impositions or juxtapositions of screens: still according to Riegl's categories, they permit the advent of pure optical surfaces. Instead of having his attention caught by tactile stimuli, instead of wishing to seize the three-dimensional forms of which the painting creates an illusion, or being seduced by the display of an interior fiction of the image, the spectator is kept firmly on the outside by these brilliant cliffs of screens which develop surface relationships and thereby magnify the pictorial plane. The risk of being absorbed by the image is averted and the gaze doubly liberated: rhythmical expansion leads the gaze beyond the frame of the painting; the folds and screens hold the gaze at a distance.

Finally, by these two routes, the spectator is required to arrange his or her own perception, endlessly combining the relationship between the forms. Accountability returns, and extends naturally from the pictorial surface to the surrounding space.

10

Delight and enjoyment are accompanied by demands that may be shot through with distress. The 'stratagem of the fabric with variable geometry', in Pierre Schneider's words,[63] far from suppressing or disguising tensions, exposes them powerfully. Above and beyond blissful enjoyment, the gaze has to deal with specifically modern ideas about the nature of the process of producing images.

Most of the time Matisse employs his fabrics, whose softness allows them to adapt to the shape of the objects they cover, in ways that are at odds with their normal usage. In *Still-life with Geraniums* (fig. 34) the large central hanging extends strangely forwards from the background – the studio wall – slashing the depth of the painting in two while at the same time giving it strong emphasis. In *Spanish Still-life* (fig. 36) the powerful two-dimensional expanse of Spanish carpet, transformed into a wall of Islamic tiles, covers only half of the sofa; the other half is painted in perspective, according to the rules that govern the creation of an illusion of depth. In *The Painter's Family* (fig. 11) the same principle is employed: the Afghan carpet on the floor follows the pictorial plane, supporting chairs, a stool and a chequerboard drawn in perspective. This aggressive juxtaposition of form with form is valid for the rule of absolute surface, and also for the rule of infinite relationship. The rhythmical repetition of pattern does not inhabit an unequivocal decorative universe; patterns are displayed in such a way that, once again, the ambiguous relationship between the referential value of the pattern as such and the pure rhythms that emerge from the spaces between the patterns is *deliberate*. The systematic intertwining of the plants and the textile designs based on plant forms in the three still-lifes discussed above is an excellent illustration of this ambiguity. The spectator is inevitably challenged on the nature of the figurative impulse and the way it is overstepped.

Undoubtedly what Matisse gained first from his interpretation of Islamic textiles was the promise of grace, in images, which springs from the mitigation of their ontological weight. 'What remains belongs to God': the artist is able to find the beauty of an evening sky in a scrap of Persian carpet simply because life shapes and reshapes itself ceaselessly, sliding from the world of nature to the world of the image, now that the shackles of imitation have been broken, now that figurative activity is no longer reliant on the need to prove that it exists.

For centuries, Western tradition had thought of the image in terms of a mirror, following the dualist paradigm of reflector and reflection. With the encouragement of Islamic art, Matisse suddenly experienced the metamorphosis of the image into an independent, decorated surface. The mirror was succeeded by the veil (a veil represents the visible as such, and inhibits speculation about the figurability of the deepest layers of being); the reflection (in the West, a melancholy symbol of metaphysical deficiency) was succeeded by the pure, immediate presence of a formal energy, welcoming to life.

On these premises, the Islamic aesthetic in textiles embodies a paradoxical glorification of impermanence: in which the most dazzling formal invention is entropied in daily use, and thereby assumes the nature of a transitory object; and in which the most perfect geometry, rather than consisting of a crystalline, intangible unity, follows the 'kaleidoscopic' impulse (to borrow an expression coined by Ernst Kühnel)[64]

Fig. 36
Henri Matisse, **Spanish Still-life**, 1910–11. Oil on canvas, 89 × 116 cm.
The State Hermitage Museum, St Petersburg

towards constant fragmentation and recomposition.

Thanks to this ambivalence, Islamic fabrics and carpets were well suited (possibly better than any other tradition) to help Matisse 'jump over the ditch',[65] encouraging him to conjoin decorative practice with critical thought about the nature of images. In Islam, this impermanence is the native land of form, eventually leading to God. For his part, Matisse maintains it as a question that, with all its initial tension, concurrently confers upon his images their impulse and threatens to tear their admirable fabric. Their paradoxical strength lies in a sort of critical decoration, inseparable from a never-ending reflection on the condition of its own existence.

Translated by Caroline Beamish

Fig. 37
Wall tile from Turkey (Iznik), late fifteenth–early sixteenth centuries. Ceramic, 37.5 × 29.5 cm. Exhibited in Paris in 1903. Musée des Art Décoratifs, Paris. Formerly in the Maciet Collection

Fig. 38
Panels from the royal bath-house, Alhambra, Granada, Spain, fourteenth century. Ceramic and stucco. Depicted in a postcard belonging to Matisse. Matisse Archives, Paris

1 For the Arabic adjective bāqī ('durable', 'without end') attributed to God in Muslim theology, see Gimaret 1988, pp. 175–82.

2 See Grabar 1973, p. 287. The author excludes the idea of any causal relationship between the development of an aesthetic and Muslim theology: 'Such an explanation does not ascribe causes: at best, it is structural in the sense that the manner of thinking about religion and the manner of thinking about the decorative arts have certain postulates in common.'

3 Clévenot 1994.

4 Kühnel 1949, p. 9. For his part, Louis Massignon defines the arabesque as a 'kind of indefinite negation of closed geometrical forms' (Massignon 1921, p. 15).

5 See Grabar 1973, p. 105, and Clévenot 1994, p. 146. The covering of the Kaaba, the kiswa, later became a piece of black silk embroidered with calligraphy in silver and gold, woven in Egypt.

6 See Grabar 1973, p. 248. On the Fatimid tirâz – both a type of fabric and the workshops in which these were produced under the authority of the caliph – see Anna Contadini and Georgette Cornu in Paris 1998, pp. 79–81 and pp. 200–3.

7 Migeon 1903B, p. 30. Migeon, then curator of the department of objets d'art at the Louvre and a great champion of Islamic art, exemplifies the close ties that then existed between Islamic art and textile aesthetics: in 1907, with Henri Saladin he published the first guide to Islamic art in France (Migeon 1907) and in 1909 a general history of textiles (Migeon 1909).

8 Lavoix 1878, p. 770.

9 Migeon 1903B, p. 3.

10 See for example Migeon 1903A, p. 4 ('It may perhaps be in the carpets and fabrics that the decorative artists will find the most to think about here'); and Cox 1900, p. 11 ('We think it necessary to present a few reflections of a very general kind, to start with on the aspirations peculiar to the oriental mind and those peculiar to the occidental mind. It was from contact between the two, encouraged by conquest and commercial expansion, that the different styles were to be born').

11 The Musée d'Art et d'Industrie de la Chambre de Commerce de Lyon was inaugurated on 6 March 1864; after 1885, its new director Antonin Terme caused the collection to specialise in textiles, hoping to make it 'the leading museum of fabrics in the world'. The new exhibition rooms were inaugurated on 28 May 1891, and a new name established: Musée Historique des Tissus de la Chambre de Commerce de Lyon (see Cox 1900, p. 111).

12 The Musée du Louvre first assigned a special room to the Islamic collection in 1905 (the former French ceramics room on the first floor of the North Wing of the old Louvre). This development can be ascribed to pressure from Gaston Migeon, as well as to competition with the Union Centrale des Arts Décoratifs, whose museum opened in the Pavillon de Marsan in the same year.

13 See Roxburgh 2000, pp. 9–38, and Labrusse 1998, pp. 275–311.

14 Riegl 1893, p. 30.

15 Riegl 1893, p. 37.

16 These were the subject of his first book, in the context of the first serious exhibition devoted to Islamic carpets (Riegl 1891). See also his short study of the Coptic fabrics which had recently come into the museum's collection (Riegl 1889).

17 Riegl 1893, p. 4.

18 Riegl 1891, p. 214.

19 Riegl 1893, p. 10 and p. 214; see also Riegl 1891, pp. 154–6 ('die durchgängige Tendenz zur abstrakten Durchbildung und Ausgestaltung der von der späten Antike überlieferten, vielfach noch an vegetabilische Formen anklingenden Elemente').

20 Riegl 1893, pp. 244–5.

21 Riegl 1898, p. 182.

22 This was thanks to the almost accidental discovery, in the attics of the Wittelsbach palace in Munich, of a group of seventeenth-century Persian carpets, known as 'Polish carpets', which formed the backbone of the exhibition (Sarre and Martin 1910, second edition, p. 32). These carpets, numbers 65–8 and 82–5 in the catalogue, were exhibited in the first room of the exhibition (see Sarre and Martin 1910, third edition, pp. 24–6). Among the 3,572 catalogue entries, 230 were carpets (nos 1–229, Sarre and Martin 1910, pp. 17–37) and 737 textiles (nos 2,232–2,968, Sarre and Martin 1910, pp. 182–218), confirming that textiles were given by far the most important role (see Moriz Dreger, 'Die Stoffe', in Sarre and Martin 1912, vol. 3, p. XII: 'Neben den Teppichen sind es wohl die Stoffe gewesen, die das aüssere Bild der Ausstellung beherrscht haben').

23 Sarre and Martin 1912, vol. III, pp. I, IV. In the same spirit, at the end of his life Kühnel also talked about the basic 'musicality' of the arabesque: 'Ein derartiges Musizieren mit dem Zeichenstift … musste für den schaffenden Geist einen unendlichen Reiz haben' (Kühnel 1949, p. 6).

24 'Muhammedanische Kunst', in Sarre and Martin 1910, second edition, p. 53, and third edition, p. 11.

25 On these aspects, see Rémi Labrusse in Rome 1997, pp. 358–62. In a letter to Marguerite Duthuit, written from Berlin on 23 May 1931, Mathilde Purrmann describes the 'muddle of Persian fragments' to be found in the 'small apartment in rue Denfert-Rochereau' where she lived with her husband before the war (Matisse Archives, Paris).

26 Riegl 1901, p. 3.

27 Matisse 1908, trans. in Flam 1995, p. 43.

28 See the letter from Odilon Redon to Matisse, 3 February 1909: 'I received your letter, but I did not wait for it to read your work; thank you all the same. I really appreciated your article; it is so lucid and written at such a calm pace' (Matisse Archives, Paris).

29 See Gloria Groom in Chicago 1994, pp. 325–8.

30 Letter to Charles Waltner, 12 April 1910, in Redon 1923, p. 91.

31 Signac 1899, p. 149.

32 Henri-Edmond Cross, letter to Henri Matisse, September–October 1908 (Matisse Archives, Paris). Cross was reacting to a photograph sent to him by Matisse.

33 Denis 1905, p. 96.

34 Puy 1910, p. 36.

35 Scherb 1910, p. 59.

36 Louis Vauxcelles, Gil Blas, Paris, 20 March 1906, quoted in Paris 1993, p. 73.

37 Matisse 1947, trans. in Flam 1995, p. 178. See also his interview with Brother Rayssiguier on 9 January 1949: 'The Orient saved us, he says, mentioning the carpets he saw in Munich (in the exhibition of Islamic art) and which are some of the things he still remembers to this day' (Matisse, Couturier and Rayssiguier 1993, p. 130).

38 A small group of Coptic, Sassanian and Byzantine fabrics were shown in the Munich exhibition (Sarre and Martin 1910, third edition, nos 2,232–2,252, pp. 182–4).

39 Demaison 1907, p. 29. This exhibition was part of a wider project: in 1906 Japanese fabrics were exhibited as well, and also French fabrics from the Middle Ages onwards.

40 Jean-Louis Vaudoyer mentions 'not less than 250 pieces, Bursa silks and Scutari velvets for the most part, but also some magnificent Persian fabrics and some silk and wool carpets which are as rare as they are seductive' (Vaudoyer 1907, p. 52). For Kelekian, see also Shreve Simpson 2000, pp. 91–112.

41 Sarre and Martin 1910, third edition, nos 2,446–2,525, p. 207 in particular. See also Kühnel 1910, p. 247 (who also mentions nearly two hundred Bursa silks lent by Kelekian). In a conversation with Fereshteh Daftari, Pierre Matisse dates his father's encounter with Kelekian to between 1907 and 1912 (Daftari 1991, p. 234). At the same time, the Armenian dealer often emphasised in his writings the modernity of Persian art, especially

to young people who, like Matisse, discovered as they roamed the museums that 'all the principles, without exception, of this art that is more than seven centuries old meet their own, contemporary needs' (Kelekian 1909, p. 11).

42 See Spurling 1998, pp. 355–6.

43 Osthaus had begun to build up the oriental collections of the Folkwang Museum in 1899 in Algeria, Tunisia and Constantinople; Coptic fabrics were added to the Persian ceramics, Mamluk lamps, Turkish carpets and Hispano-Moorish ceramics (see Osthaus 1971, pp. 93, 187, 190). Osthaus was a member of the working party for the Islamic exhibition in Munich in 1910.

44 After Piotr Shchukin's suicide, Matisse wrote to Sergei: 'It was with sadness that I learned of the death of your elder brother, whom I had seen so busy with his collection' (letter of 17 November 1912, Matisse Archives, Paris). In 1934 again, on the subject of Russian folk embroidery, Matisse confided to Alexander Romm: 'I studied the book on embroidery you sent to me with interest. I had already seen this kind of work in Moscow in the national art museum set up by the brother of Sergei Ivanovich Shchukin' (letter of 14 February 1934, quoted in Leningrad 1969, p. 132). Like Osthaus, Piotr Shchukin was a member of the working party for the exhibition of Islamic art held in Munich in 1910.

45 See Labrusse 1998, pp. 283–5.

46 Loeb 1945, p. 66.

47 Letter to Isabella Stewart Gardner from Munich, 7 August 1910, quoted in Labrusse 1999, p. 105.

48 Handwritten note on the flyleaf of a copy of the catalogue of the Munich exhibition, in the Bibliothèque Byzantine (Thomas Whittemore Collection), Paris. This must be the early seventeenth-century Persian tunic now in the Osterreichisches Museum für Kunst und Industrie, Vienna (Sarre and Martin, 1910, third edition, no. 2,369, p. 199). On Whittemore, see Labrusse and Podzemskaia 2000.

49 Fry 1910, pp. 83–4.

50 See Tschudi 1996, p. 260.

51 See the letter from Sergei Shchukin to Ilya Ostrooukhov, written from Cairo on 10 November 1909, on the subject of Matisse: 'Chudi told me himself that he is one of the most important painters of this century' (quoted in Kostenevich and Semenova 1993, p. 178).

52 Letter to Matisse of 27 June 1910, in Tschudi 1996, p. 260. Tschudi had commissioned a still-life from Matisse in October 1909, when he first visited the studio. After a second visit, in January 1910, and despite Matisse's attempt to sell him the portrait of a girl, he stuck by his first choice: 'I willingly accept your offer to send me the portrait of the girl again, in order to study it closely. It is true, I only saw it in haste and I certainly have not yet appreciated its merit. I do ask you however to include the first still-life which, so far, has made the greatest impression on me' (letter of 22 February 1910, Matisse Archives, Paris).

53 See the letter from Shchukin to Matisse (who was then in Spain) of 14 November 1910: 'Yesterday I saw a painter from Munich, Mr Kandinsky, and he hugely admired your still-life which is with Mr Chud' (quoted in Kostenevich and Semenova 1993, pp. 167–8).

54 Conversations with Pierre Courthion, 1941 (Matisse Archives, Paris).

55 Letter to Sergei Shchukin of 1 February 1912, quoted in Labrusse 1999, pp. 208–9.

56 Letter to Amélie Matisse, 31 December 1918 (Matisse Archives, Paris).

57 Letter from Marguerite Matisse to her father, 25 November 1920 (Matisse Archives, Paris).

58 On Matisse's trip to Polynesia in 1930, see Le Cateau-Cambrésis 1998.

59 Matisse must have discovered these fabrics at the beginning of the 1920s through André Level, a friend since 1904 (see Henri Clouzot, Tissus nègres, Librairie des Arts Décoratifs, Paris, undated, unpaginated; the

author was a curator at the Musée Galliéra in Paris at the time. He tells how, having discovered a collection of these fabrics in Antwerp in 1921, he communicated his enthusiasm to André Level). A Kuba fabric from Matisse's collection was published in Cahiers d'art in 1927 (Christian Zervos, 'L'Art nègre', Cahiers d'art, Paris, 1927, nos 7–8, p. 229).

60 See the letter to Amélie Matisse from Granada, 11 December 1910: 'In Madrid I bought a very pretty white carpet with blue patterns, not in very good condition, but I think I shall use it a lot in my work. Cost 50 F. It is cream with dark-blue patterns. This is what it looks like [sketch]. It might be about 2 m × 1.8 m. It could be a good door covering. It is in beautiful bouclé wool, short pile. This is about the size of the loops [sketch]. I had never seen anything like it. It caught my eye in an antique shop in Madrid. I was amazed to see some here too, but much more expensive, up to 300 pesetas. It seems that foreigners love them. They have been made in the Sierra Nevada for more than 100 years. Every young girl would make a carpet like this for her trousseau, to cover the floor, and the same kind of thing to cover her bed but in silk' (Matisse Archives, Paris).

61 See his letter to his wife from Granada, written at the end of December 1910: 'The Alhambra is a marvel. I felt a great surge of emotion when I was there' (Matisse Archives, Paris).

62 Moriz Dreger, 'Die Stoffe', in Sarre and Martin 1912, p. 1.

63 Schneider 2001, p. 371.

64 Kühnel 1949, p. 7.

65 Matisse 1947, trans. in Flam 1995, p. 178: 'You surrender yourself that much better when you see your efforts confirmed by such an ancient tradition. It helps you jump over the ditch.'

Chasubles: 'The Purest and Most Radiant Works Ever Created by Matisse'

DOMINIQUE SZYMUSIAK

'In 1952, when I saw Matisse for the last time in his studio in Nice,' wrote Alfred H. Barr, Director of the Museum of Modern Art in New York,[1] 'there were twenty or so *maquettes* for chasubles pinned to the wall like giant butterflies. I can well understand Picasso's enthusiasm. They seemed to me to be among the purest and most radiant works ever created by Matisse.'[2] Barr is referring to Picasso's visit to Matisse a few months earlier, in June 1951.[3] Picasso had seen the *maquettes* while showing Matisse ten of his landscape paintings. As Hélène Adant's photographs reveal (fig. 39), Matisse placed Picasso's *Paysage de Vallauris* (1951) over the fireplace in his bedroom-studio, in the centre of the wall on which he had pinned the *maquettes* seen by Picasso.

The conception of the *maquettes* for the chasubles began when the Dominican chapel in Vence, on which Matisse had been working for three years, was nearly finished. In a letter dated 31 October 1950, Matisse sought the advice of Father Couturier, instigator of an important revival of religious art in the postwar period. Father Couturier had assisted with designs for the chapel from the outset. After the daunting task of designing stained-glass windows and ceramics, the cutting out of chasubles from sheets of paper painted with gouache must have proved a joyful interlude. The white-and-gold chasuble was needed for the inauguration ceremony of the chapel in June 1951. Matisse wrote to Father Couturier about the choice of fabrics: 'taffeta, velveteen…'. Having spent his childhood among textiles manufactured for the top end of the market, Matisse was familiar with the characteristics of different types of fabric: 'I need your advice about liturgical vestments. What colours should chasubles be? Where in Paris do you think I could find taffeta and velveteen to make them from?'[4] Father Couturier replied: 'The colours of the different chasubles are white, green, red, purple, black and, if you like, for very important ceremonies, gold. These various fabrics can be found in specialised shops and are generally of good quality, but the colours are not always attractive. It would be better to go to ordinary silk factories where there is more choice: Bianchini-Férier is expensive, but has beautiful things.'[5]

Fig. 39
Hélène Adant, Matisse's bedroom at the Hotel Régina, Nice, c. 1952.
On the wall: maquettes of chasubles for the Vence chapel.
On the mantelpiece: Picasso's *Paysage de Vallauris*, 1951, on loan to Matisse.
Photograph. Musée National d'Art Moderne, Centre Georges Pompidou, Paris

Fig. 40
Henri Matisse, Green chasuble, maquette of front view, 1950–51. Gouache on paper, cut and pasted, 126.5 × 198 cm. Musée Matisse, Nice-Cimiez

Fig. 41
Henri Matisse, Green chasuble, maquette of back view, 1950–51. Gouache on paper, cut and pasted, 131.7 × 197.5 cm. Musée Matisse, Nice-Cimiez

For the third time in his career, Matisse was creating costumes, not for a ballet now, but for religious ceremonies. In a similar way to earlier commissions, the performance was fixed and he was to design the décor. These liturgical vestments represented a grand finale, and were intended to harmonise with the architecture of the chapel, which was by then almost complete. Matisse used his previous experience to give him guidance. In 1919, at the request of Sergei Diaghilev, he created coats in the form of copes for Chinese mandarins, the Emperor of China and his chamberlain in the ballet *Le Chant du rossignol* (with music by Igor Stravinsky and choreography by Léonide Massine). He undertook the costumes for another ballet, *Le Rouge et le noir* (*L'Etrange Farandole*), with choreography again by Massine and music by Shostakovich, in 1938. 'I had a backdrop divided into four colours, blue, red, black and yellow, with white arcs. I dressed my dancers in the colours of the scenery, skin-tight costumes in blue, red, yellow and white.'[6] Matisse's idea of skin-tight costumes was startlingly innovative. Each group of dancers wore a different colour, and each costume was decorated with the shapes of either seaweed or flames, appliquéd in contrasting matt and shiny fabrics.

In the Roman Catholic liturgy, the role of the chasuble is to clothe the celebrant in a dignified and impressive fashion for each religious service. The officiating priest is not the actor in a play; rather he is administering a rite which has transcendental implications. The chasuble clothes the officiating priest and also contributes to the aesthetic impact of the ceremony; throughout the priest has to spread his arms wide, kneel and bend, and also move around the altar in a preordained ritual.

Father Couturier sent Matisse some examples of chasubles which the painter found 'very attractive'[7] and, a few days later, a pattern for the back on which he had marked in red the shortest side of the front. Couturier modernised the cut, using a shape favoured in the late Middle Ages – a type of great cloak cut into two semicircles – in contrast to the traditional chasuble, which is narrow like a violin case. These chasubles were based on the Roman travelling cloak, the *paenula*, and provided a much more impressive fullness. Each chasuble consisted of two parts, front and back, stitched at the top. Two metres wide and one metre thirty centimetres long, they covered the celebrant from head to toe. In preparation for his task, Matisse asked to see an eighteenth-century cloak belonging to a knight of the Ordre du Saint-Esprit while on a private visit with Father Couturier to the exhibition 'L'Art et la vie au Moyen Age à travers les blasons et les sceaux' at the Hôtel de Soubise in Paris. The cloak in question was embroidered with a constellation of gold flames against a dark background, borrowed from a fifteenth-century example.

In his white-painted studio in Nice, Matisse made twenty *maquettes*, but kept only the twelve he needed for the production of six chasubles. He made the first *maquette* for the white-and-gold chasuble by taking some paper painted in lemon-yellow gouache – the same yellow he had used for the stained-glass windows – and cutting out the shape of a tree. It seems astonishing that he should have chosen a tree, with all its pagan connotations, to decorate a vestment made for religious purposes. The tree is linked with the legend of Daphne, one of humankind's fundamental myths, according to Pierre Schneider;[8] it tells the story of a human being absorbed into the plant world and transformed into a tree. Matisse built up the branches to the central axis and filled the white space of the background by gradually adding scraps of golden-yellow paper, to which he had added white shapes to create empty spaces 'filled' with light. He

designed a chasuble made of light, of the light that emanates from the stained-glass windows and from the black-and-white ceramics, and which also shines forth from the priestly garments. Although it never progressed beyond the stage of *maquette*, the pure combination of white with the lemon yellow of the leaves in this design produces an atmosphere of spirituality and poetry.

The lack of any cross, however, obliged Matisse to start afresh. His second *maquette* is scattered with quatrefoil flowers in the tradition of the embroidered chasuble. The painter created a decorative space with which he was not satisfied, as he went on to compose a third version. The motif on the final version of this chasuble, designed for the great festivals of the Christian year, consists of a stylised yellow-and-green appliquéd plant with fruit and flowers for the front, and a chalice and the Eucharist for the back. The arc described by the design follows the garment's shape, and the chasuble illuminates the priest in the sacred space of the chapel in a way that chimes with the spirituality emanating from the building itself.

In his diary Father Couturier records Matisse's impressions of a visit to Notre-Dame in Paris the previous summer. 'The huge crowd, heads as far as the eye could see, the architecture, the stained glass and, now and again, waves of organ music flowing over our heads, made a great impression. When I came out, I said to myself: "Well! Compared with all that, what does the chapel add up to?" Then I thought: "It's a flower. It's only a flower, but it is a flower." '9 The first *maquette* uses a tree as its theme; subsequent *maquettes* adopt floral symbolism: the palm, seaweed, the leaf. The chasubles' iconography, sustained by the consonance of certain colours, combines to transform the figure of the celebrant into a homage to creation.

A green chasuble is worn for the majority of the

Fig. 42
Henri Matisse, Green chalice cloth, *maquette*, 1950–51. Gouache on paper, cut and pasted, 52.7 × 53 cm. Musée Matisse, Nice-Cimiez

Fig. 43
Henri Matisse, White chalice cloth, *maquette*, 1950–51. Gouache on paper, cut and pasted, 52.7 × 53 cm. Musée Matisse, Nice-Cimiez

Fig. 44
Henri Matisse, Violet chalice cloth, *maquette*, 1950–51. Gouache on paper, cut and pasted, 52.7 × 52.7 cm. Musée Matisse, Nice-Cimiez

Fig. 45
Henri Matisse, Black chalice cloth, *maquette*, 1950–51. Gouache on paper, cut and pasted, 51.4 × 51.4 cm. Musée Matisse, Nice-Cimiez

liturgical year. The colour symbolises redemption and the hope for birth into the life of the spirit. Spiky yellow shapes are placed on black squares. Jagged flames emerge from the black with the same intensity used to suggest the baleful sky from which Icarus falls in Matisse's book *Jazz* (1947). Light in the dark night, against a background of hope – the priest wears a glimmer of hope for humanity.

The pattern on the pink chasuble, to be worn on feast days, consists of stars, flowers and seaweed, appliquéd to blue rectangles on the front and blue quatrefoils on the back. They recall the small Gothic windows set in a quatrefoil framework of stone. A crown of thorns, with its connotations of religious art, stands out in contrast.

On a few days in the year the priest wears a red chasuble to associate himself with Christ's Passion and the sufferings of the martyrs. 'While he was designing it, Matisse had in his mind's eye a small sun-kissed island set amid warm seas (poppy red), with scorched vegetation (reeds and yellow bamboos) and pullulating with mosquitoes (small black crosses) to make life unbearable, to torment you.'[10] The violence of the red in accord with the stridency of the yellow produces an overwhelming impact, even though the pattern itself comes from insignificant sources and might have occupied a purely decorative role. In that case it would have contrasted with the representation of compassion for human suffering. Matisse felt that 'red is a colour that "stings" and has no flat plane; it jabs you in the eye'.[11] This chasuble should be considered exceptional in the context of the chapel, as red is absent from the components of the architecture, and is only apparent when the sun shines through the windows onto the floor at certain times of day. Pink and purple also appear in the building only as reflected light.

The purple chasuble, to be worn at times of penitence, is scattered with green flowers and blue butterflies.

Matisse had bought some blue morph butterflies in the rue de Rivoli in 1898 and recalled their magnificent blue in a letter to his wife from Tahiti thirty years later. Once again the combination of purple with blue and green set him dreaming of certain light values, to which he attached a dream of butterflies and flowers, liberty and beauty, rather than of penitence.

The most problematic chasubles for Matisse were the black ones to be worn at funerals. He made seven different *maquettes*, and was excited by the juxtaposition

Fig. 46
Hélène Adant, Priest wearing the pink chasuble, chapel in Vence. Photograph

Fig. 47
Hélène Adant, Priest wearing the white chasuble, chapel in Vence. Photograph

background. Four series of *maquettes* were created in succession.

The first comprised only a cross inscribed in the shape of a 'v' and a constellation of stars made with superimposed rectangles of paper. The second was based on the word 'Esperlucat'. Matisse wrote on a photograph, 'Composition born of the desire to harvest the corn [*faire du blé*], and following my encounter with a Provençal word meaning "to have one's eyes opened" – to see or to notice. If you think about a mortuary chasuble, you realise that the most reassuring way to meet death is to be accompanied by one's good works (*blé*).'[12]

He designed two other *maquettes* with seaweed and fish dancing against a black background, giving a feeling of freedom. Their compositions follow the circular shape of the chasuble, going around it in perpetual motion. Probably in order to return to the peaceful feeling of serenity, Matisse composed a final version, with a design of monumental wings around the letters of 'Esperlucat', with a white circle on the front and a single cross on the back; this gives a feeling of great calm. While the previous project was composed very freely against the black ground, the final version, with its vertical pattern, symmetrical axis and the very pronounced curve of the garment's drop, gives an impression of peace. Father Couturier notes in his diary: 'We spoke of the black chasuble. I said that it was not a gloomy chasuble, it was a chasuble for resurrection. He replied: "That's what you need, isn't it? Death is not the end of everything, it's the opening of a door." As he said this, his eyes filled with tears.'[13]

The six chasubles were to be accompanied by the accessories needed for Roman Catholic worship. This group of items was made with special care by the Dominican sisters of Crépieux, near Lyons, who specialised in liturgical vestments.[14] The fabric chosen

of white forms on a black background, and by their relationship with the colours of the stained-glass windows, 'a surface of light and colour'. Whereas the black drawings on a white background used in the chapel's wall tiles leave plenty of space between the lines of the drawing, the *maquettes* for the chasubles reveal the white of the patterns not with a gouge, as in a linocut, but by cut white paper being glued to the black was silk poplin, which gives a smooth finish similar to that of the gouache in the maquettes. All the chasubles were lined in colour – very pale yellow for the white chasuble; yellow for the green and red chasubles; mauve for the purple chasuble; very pale pink for the pink chasuble; and white for the black chasuble – and this plays an important role as the linings are visible during the Mass.

The sometimes violent brilliance of their colours and the skilful techniques involved in making the chasubles accentuate the sacred meaning of the liturgy. During a service, while wearing a robe whose pure colour is enhanced by the contrasting colours of its patterns, the priest, through his vestment, adds another note to the symphony of blues, greens and yellows in the stained-glass windows. Part of the choreography of the liturgical event, he is its embodiment in the intense luminosity of the chapel. '"With regard to the chapel", he said to me, "I have created a religious space."

'Visit to Matisse – he tells me that he definitely prefers El Greco to Velázquez, the latter being too perfect, too knowledgeable: "It's like a very beautiful fabric, a very handsome marble." But in El Greco there is soul everywhere, "right down to the hooves of St Martin's horse".

'"I am inhabited by things that wake me but do not reveal themselves." '[15]

Translated by Caroline Beamish

1 The maquettes for the red chasuble were shown in 'Henri Matisse', an exhibition organised by Alfred H. Barr at the Museum of Modern Art, New York, from November 1951 to January 1952, before a tour to Cleveland, Chicago and San Francisco.
2 Paris 1989, p. 393.
3 Matisse, Couturier and Rayssiguier 1993; diary of Father Couturier dated 23 June 1951, p. 398.
4 Letter from Matisse to Father Couturier, 31 October 1950, in Matisse, Couturier and Rayssiguier 1993, p. 373.
5 Letter from Father Couturier to Matisse, 4 November 1950, in Matisse, Couturier and Rayssiguier 1993, p. 375.
6 Pierre Schneider, Matisse, Paris, 1984, p. 523.
7 Letter from Matisse to Father Couturier, 22 November 1950, in Matisse, Couturier and Rayssiguier 1993, p. 377: 'Yesterday I saw Mother Françoise, director of Blanche de Castille. She brought me your chasubles: very attractive, I should like to make these vestments – and I am taking advantage of the repose I need after my journey to pursue this peaceful occupation.'
8 See Matisse et l'arbre, Pierre Schneider, exh. cat., Musée Matisse, Le Cateau-Cambrésis, 2003, pp. 148–60.
9 Diary of Father Couturier, 8 March 1952, in Matisse, Couturier and Rayssiguier 1993, p. 420.
10 Lydia Delectorskaya, quoted in Les Chasubles de Matisse, exh. cat., Musée Matisse, Le Cateau-Cambrésis, 1997.
11 Brother Rayssiguier's interview with Henri Matisse, 12 June 1949, in Matisse, Couturier and Rayssiguier 1993, p. 205.
12 Les Chapelles du Rosaire à Vence par Matisse et de Notre-Dame-du-Haut à Ronchamp par Le Corbusier, Paris, 1955, ill. 46, 'Etudes pour les chasubles avec annotations de la main de Matisse'.
13 Diary of Father Couturier, 13 March 1952, in Matisse, Couturier and Rayssiguier 1993, p. 420.
14 In 1996 identical copies of the chasubles and their accessories were made on the initiative of Sister Jacques-Marie and Lydia Delectorskaya.
15 Diary of Father Couturier, 17 July 1951, in Matisse, Couturier and Rayssiguier 1993, p. 401.

Overleaf
Page 70
Toile de Jouy, early nineteenth century
Cotton, 155 × 172 cm
Private collection

Page 71
Chinese silk coverlet, probably eighteenth century
Silk, 283 × 236 cm
Private collection

Page 72, top left
A length of red-and-yellow woven cloth, possibly from Cambodia or Bali, late nineteenth century
Woven cloth, 185 × 96 cm
Private collection

Page 72, top right
Chinese silk coverlet, probably eighteenth century (see also p. 71)
Silk, 283 × 236 cm
Private collection

Page 72, bottom left
Moroccan sash worn around a man's waist, nineteenth century
Silk, 113 × 113 cm
Private collection

Page 72, bottom right
Moroccan embroidered silk, nineteenth century
Silk, 178 × 53 cm
Private collection

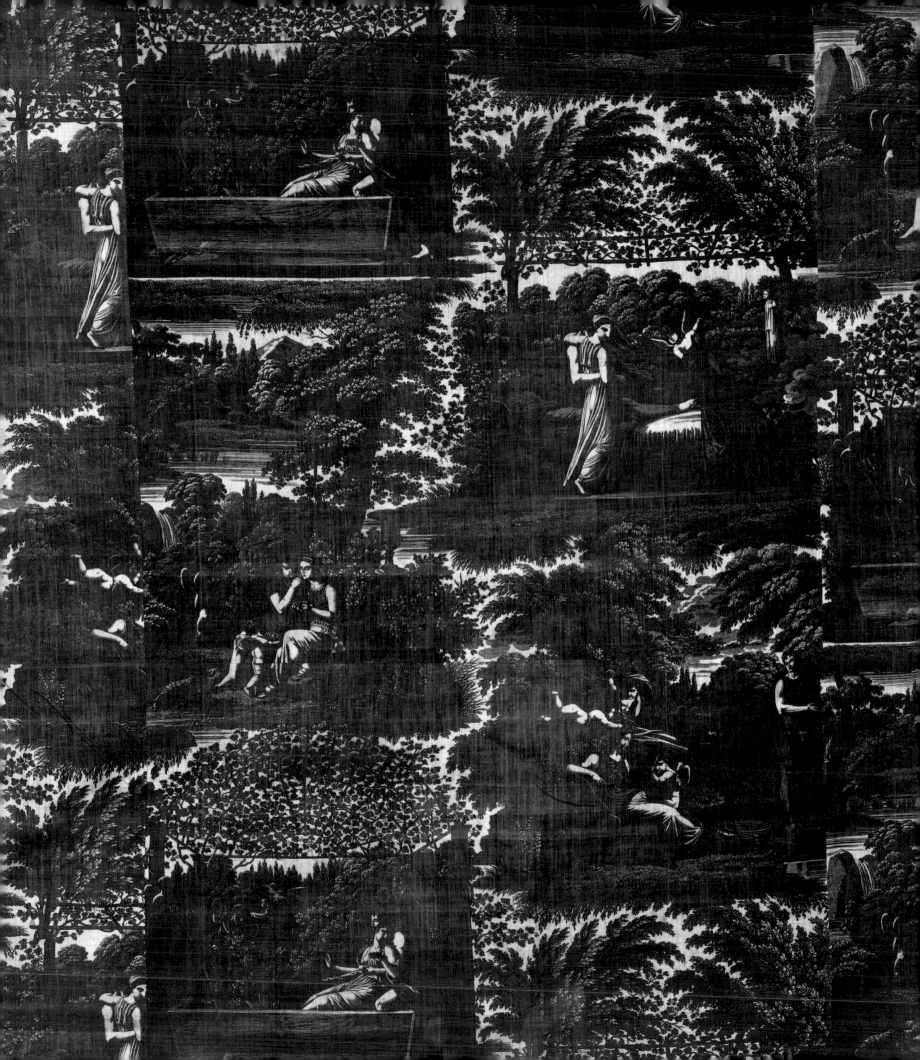

Catalogue plates

Beginnings in Bohain

Textiles were fundamental to Matisse's artistic vision from his very early days to the end of his long life at the age of eighty-four. He was born in 1869 in the small town of Le Cateau-Cambrésis and brought up some twenty miles away at Bohain-en-Vermandois in the flat, rainy terrain of Picardy in northern France. Since the Middle Ages the region had been a centre for the manufacture of textiles, linen, wool and silk. By the end of the nineteenth century, when Matisse was growing up, Bohain was renowned as a producer of luxury fabrics – embossed and patterned velvet, tulle, voile and, above all, silk – and was pre-eminent in supplying the top end of the Paris fashion trade. Matisse father's family were weavers and the weavers' workshops that were to be found throughout Bohain would have been an everyday aspect of his childhood. He would have seen emerging from their looms materials made to designs of astonishing originality, often in eye-catching and unconventional colour combinations. The weavers of Bohain were celebrated for their bold experimentation. The luxury textile industry in Bohain declined throughout the twentieth century and eventually disappeared. However, the surviving pattern books, examples of which are displayed in the exhibition, give an idea of the variety and inventiveness of these sumptuous fabric designs, ranging from the complex and floral motifs of the 1880s to the more geometric and abstract patterns of the 1890s.

It is not surprising that textile design was one of the principal subjects taught at the local municipal art school, the Ecole Quentin de La Tour in St-Quentin, where Matisse enrolled for drawing classes. Matisse had found his artistic vocation suddenly, and quite late, when, at the age of twenty, he was convalescing from a bout of pneumonia and his mother gave him a box of paints. In marked contrast to the creative freedom of the local weavers, teaching at the art school adhered to the most conservative standards of the moribund Beaux-Arts system. Drawing from plaster casts was emphasised. Matisse also taught himself painting techniques by copying reproductions and by imitating traditional subjects, such as still-life in the Dutch seventeenth-century manner (cat. 1). It did not take Matisse long to realise that he had little to learn from such a system. By contrast, his early exposure to fabric design had a lasting impact. As this exhibition demonstrates, it gave him a profound appreciation of abstract pattern and a radical sense of the way in which colour could function, leading him occasionally to transpose the entire colour basis of a painting, just as textile weavers create the same design in different colourways. AD

Opposite
Detail of a silk sample book from Bohain-en-Vermandois, 1906

Overleaf
Silk sample books from Bohain-en-Vermandois, 1906 (p. 76, top), 1891 (p. 76, bottom), 1900 (p. 77, top), 1906 (p. 77, bottom)

Cat. 1
Still-life, Books and Candle, 1890
Oil on canvas, 38.1 × 36 cm
Musée de Pontoise

Cat. 2
Still-life with Schiedam, 1896
Oil on canvas, 29 × 35 cm
Musée départemental Matisse,
Le Cateau-Cambrésis

Cat. 3
Bouquet of Daisies, c. 1895
Oil on canvas, 95 × 80 cm
Musée départemental Matisse, Le Cateau-Cambrésis

Cat. 4
The Breton Weaver, 1895–96
Oil on wood, 40 × 54.5 cm
*Musée National d'Art Moderne, Centre
Georges Pompidou, Paris, on deposit
at the Musée départemental Matisse,
Le Cateau-Cambrésis*

A Balance of Forces

The length of cotton 'toile de Jouy' that Matisse spotted 'from the upper deck of an old-fashioned bus. Somewhere on the Left Bank, near the Carrefour de Buci' in 1903 was for him a talisman.[1] 'The discovery of the model, as described by Matisse, is always love at first sight. In the case of the bus journey it was for a piece of stuff hanging in a junk shop. Matisse painted with that piece of stuff for years.'[2] It proved a crucial ally in his struggle to demolish the ancient canons of perspective, tonal values and three-dimensional illusion. Matisse's evolution can be traced from the successive stages this cloth went through on his canvases, starting as a conventional prop covering a table (cat. 5) or providing a background for a figure subject (cat. 6), but then exerting increasing power as the pattern took on a life of its own in Still-life with Blue Tablecloth (1905–06; cat. 7), in which the stylised garlands and floral baskets explode in a virtually abstract display of colour. Finally, it took over altogether and in Harmony in Red (1908; fig. 2) and Still-life with Blue Tablecloth (1909; cat. 9), works that shocked Matisse's contemporaries, the textile spreads from the table across the canvas to become the motif of the whole composition.

To heighten the effect of a continuous arabesque field, Matisse took the sudden and radical step of transposing the entire colour scheme of Harmony in Red from blue to a vivid saturated red. It is a testimony to the open-mindedness of Sergei Shchukin, the Russian textile merchant who bought most of the paintings inspired by textiles from this most revolutionary phase of Matisse's career, that he was just as pleased with the red painting as with the blue one he had originally commissioned.

Matisse's taste in textiles was eclectic. Photographs taken of the different rooms in which he lived and worked show fabrics everywhere – draped over furniture, hanging on the walls, or rigged up in makeshift theatrical sets. They reveal the range that appealed to him, from traditional eighteenth- and nineteenth-century French textiles to Turkish and Moroccan robes, hats, jackets and bits of embroidery or Chinese hangings. The presence of the 'toile de Jouy' in a number of the photographs of Matisse's studio at the Villa Le Rêve at Vence taken by Hélène Adant in 1947 provides proof of its enduring meaning for Matisse throughout his life.

Opposite
French printed fabric, nineteenth century
Cotton and linen, 125 × 177 cm
Private collection

The term 'toile de Jouy', which refers to the printed cotton produced by the Oberkampf textile manufacturer at Jouy en Josas in Normandy from 1760 to 1843, is most often associated with a Rococo pattern of shepherds and shepherdesses encircled with floral garlands, usually in blue or pink on a white ground. In fact, the term is generic and encompasses a wider range of designs from Neoclassical to more generalised floral patterns. Although generally referred to as toile de Jouy in Matisse literature, the fabric Matisse owned is a later design not produced at Jouy. Its stylised dark-blue cartouches and baskets of flowers probably have their origins in an eighteenth-century design, while the closed forms of cartouches, rather than the open meandering arabesques more typical of the eighteenth century, suggest that Matisse's piece dates from the nineteenth century.[3]

The 'toile de Jouy' was the starting-point for a whole series of canvases, though the prayer-mats in red, black and yellow that he found in Algeria in 1906 were also influential, inspiring Still-life with a Red Rug (1906; fig. 9), Dishes and Fruit on a red-and-black Rug (1906; cat. 8) and the red Persian rug bought the same year. Matisse's highly tuned sense of abstract pattern was enhanced by his study of the huge display of textiles and carpets in the great Islamic exhibition held in Munich in 1910 and his discovery of Andalusian architecture and textiles in Spain later that year.   AD

1   Aragon 1972, p. 89.
2   Aragon 1972, p. 89.
3   For this information I am indebted to Clare Brown, Keeper of European Textiles at the Victoria and Albert Museum, London, Mélanie Rissel, conservateur du Musée de la Toile de Jouy en Josas, and Xavier Petitcol, Expert, Paris.

Opposite top
French woven silk, late nineteenth century
Silk, 64 × 52 cm
Private collection

Opposite bottom
French woven silk, late nineteenth century
Silk, 53 × 70 cm
Private collection

Cat. 5
Pierre Matisse with Bidouille, 1904
Oil on canvas, 73.7 × 59 cm
Private collection

Cat. 6
The Guitarist, 1903
Oil on canvas, 55 × 46 cm
Private collection, Switzerland
Courtesy of Pierre Sebastien Fine Art

Cat. 7
Still-life with Blue Tablecloth, 1905–06
Oil on canvas, 73 × 92 cm
The State Hermitage Museum, St Petersburg, inv. 7696

Cat. 8
Dishes and Fruit on a red-and-black Rug, 1906
Oil on canvas, 61 × 73 cm
The State Hermitage Museum, St Petersburg, inv. 8998

Cat. 9
Still-life with Blue Tablecloth, 1909
Oil on canvas, 88 × 118 cm
The State Hermitage Museum, St Petersburg, inv. 6569

Cat. 10
Portrait of Greta Moll, 1908
Oil on canvas, 93 × 73.4 cm
The Trustees of The National Gallery, London

Cat. 11
Seville Still-life, 1910–11
Oil on canvas, 90 × 117 cm
The State Hermitage Museum, St Petersburg, inv. 6570

Cat. 12
The Pink Studio, 1911
Oil on canvas, 179.5 × 221 cm
The Pushkin State Museum of Fine Arts, Moscow

Cat. 13
Study for **Basket of Oranges**, 1912
Pen and ink, 26 × 17.1 cm
Musée Picasso, Paris

Cat. 14
Corner of the Artist's Studio, 1912
Oil on canvas, 191.5 × 114 cm
The Pushkin State Museum of Fine Arts, Moscow

Cat. 15
Plaster Figure with Bouquet of Flowers, 1919
Oil on canvas, 113 × 87 cm
Museu de Arte de São Paolo Assis Chateaubriand, São Paolo
Formerly Leigh B. Block Collection

Cat. 16
Pansies, 1918–19
Oil on paper mounted on wood, 48.9 × 45.1 cm
The Metropolitan Museum of Art, New York,
bequest of Joan Whitney Payson, 1975 (1976.201.22)

A Decorative Art

In his work of the 1920s, often referred to as the 'Nice' period, Matisse created a fantasy world, an exotic, hot-house setting in which to display the seductive, reclining odalisques that were his principal subject during these years. He now greatly expanded his dressing-up box of costumes and textiles, attiring his models in see-through pantaloons, silken sashes and embroidered boleros that he had picked up on his visits to Morocco or from the wife of a Lebanese carpet-dealer, Mme Ibrahim, on the rue de Rivoli and various other shops in Paris. (Visitors to Matisse's Nice studio were confronted by a treasure-house crammed with rugs, cushions, folding screens heaped with patterned stuffs, carpets and wall-hangings.) As contemporary photographs reveal (p. 2), Matisse improvised an elaborate mise en scène in which a length of French Empire silk was rigged up with some Algerian embroideries, Moroccan rugs, and a vivid North African hanging that vied with the exuberantly patterned wallpaper in the artist's modest two-roomed apartment. The pierced, arcaded textiles or haitis,[1] made of pieces of coloured fabrics mounted on a length of heavy jute, in imitation of the intricately chiselled wooden screens or moucharabiehs that are found throughout the Islamic world, were intended to adorn buildings and tents for weddings and other festive occasions. Matisse owned a number of these beautiful hangings, and fixed one to a folding screen. He used them now to enrich the chromatic splendour and exotic ambience of a whole range of his paintings and lithographs of odalisques (cats 17, 18 and 27).

Matisse had visited Algeria in 1906 and was bowled over by the intense colour he discovered there. A red Algerian prayer-mat, or, more likely, a piece of red, patterned fabric, inspired two of his boldest early still-lifes (cat. 8 and fig. 9). A visit to the great exhibition of Islamic art in Munich in 1910 confirmed his deep appreciation for the abstract beauty of Muslim art, an experience that was further enhanced by visiting the Alhambra later that year on a trip to Andalusia in southern Spain and by stays in Morocco in 1912 and 1913. In Madrid, Matisse bought a cream wool coverlet with a blue motif of pomegranates from the Sierra Nevada mountains, which dominates his great Pink Studio of 1911 (cat. 12). Together with a collection of Spanish shawls, this coverlet provided the inspiration for his two spectacular

Opposite
North African haiti (pierced and appliquéd hanging),
late nineteenth or early twentieth century
Coloured cotton appliquéd to sackcloth, 190 × 129 cm
Private collection

Spanish still-lifes (cat. 11 and fig. 36) painted over the winter of 1910 to 1911 that so inspired Kandinsky.

In pursuing the orientalist theme, Matisse was heir to a well-established tradition in French painting dominated above all by Delacroix. Yet, unlike Delacroix and all the painters fascinated by the Middle East that followed him, Matisse did not sustain an impervious illusion of exoticism in his paintings, but rather made the spectator privy to his thinly disguised make-believe. During the 1920s he was fascinated by the glamorous artifice he observed in the newly developing cinema industry in Nice. Young extras were often the models for his compositions. At the end of 1930s Moroccan costumes again appear in Matisse's work, this time the long, striped kaftans, one in vivid purple with a white stripe (p. 102) and another in amber and green trimmed with gold lace that inspired a group of exuberant paintings of exotically clad models in radiant rooms filled with plants and flowers (cats 43 and 44).

Around this time, the intricate embroidery on a group of Romanian peasant blouses that Matisse had acquired from his friend Pallady led to an extensive group of paintings and drawings (cats 50, 56 and 60). It seems that these blouses enjoyed a certain vogue in Paris in the 1920s, partly owing to the fact that they were worn by the glamorous Queen Marie of Romania, and the Romanian sculptor

Constantin Brancusi was celebrated for appearing at Montparnasse parties dressed as a Romanian peasant. Matisse's drawings and paintings of his blouses show different responses to the motif. In the beautiful The Dream (1940; cat. 51) the design of the blouse emphasises the figure's boldly simplified form, echoed in some of the drawings. In other drawings Matisse's remarkable economy of line captures the delicate tracery of the blouse's embroidery.

Yet it was not only ethnic costume that appealed to Matisse. He had always been interested in high fashion and his wife and sister wore dresses by Paul Poiret's sister, Germaine Bongard. In 1938 Matisse bought dresses from end-of-season sales at the Paris couture houses in the quartier around the rue de Boétie. Again, these dresses became the starting-points for his paintings. Among the most striking gowns in his collection were two in yellow, blue and orange plaid taffeta with wide circular skirts, one with a little purple jacket (p. 107). A chic striped dress with spaghetti shoulder straps is the subject of the exuberant Asia (1946) and of a series of Themes and Variations drawings (cats 64, 65, 66, 67, 68 and 69). Matisse's drawing suggests contemporary fashion illustration in which a sophisticated model adopts a range of alluring poses familiar from contemporary fashion photographs.[2] AD

1 I am indebted for this information to Marie-France Vivier, responsable des collections et de la muséographie d'Afrique du Nord, Musée du Quai Branly, Paris.
2 See thesis by Katherine M. Bourguignon, 'Un Viol de moi-même: Matisse and the Female Model', University of Michigan, Ann Arbor, 1988, p. 199.

Opposite
North African pierced and appliquéd hanging,
late nineteenth or early twentieth century
Coloured cotton appliquéd to sackcloth,
138 × 126 cm
Private collection

Overleaf
Red pierced North African hanging,
nineteenth or early twentieth century
Coloured cotton appliquéd to sackcloth,
138 × 80 cm
Private collection

North African haiti, nineteenth or early
twentieth century
Coloured cotton appliquéd to sackcloth,
260 × 122 cm
Private collection

Ottoman striped silk robe, nineteenth century
Silk, 100 × 68 cm
Private collection

Turkish *entari* (woman's robe),
nineteenth century
Silk, 160 × 55 cm
Private collection

Ottoman or North African jacket, second half of the nineteenth century
Velvet, 50 × 118 cm
Private collection

Romanian peasant blouse, second
half of the nineteenth century
Cotton, 44 × 183 cm
Private collection

Romanian peasant blouse, second
half of the nineteenth century
Cotton, 46 × 80 cm
Private collection

Romanian peasant blouse, second
half of the nineteenth century
Cotton, 46 × 151 cm
Private collection

Detail overleaf

Parisian couture dress and jacket, 1938
Taffeta, height 170 cm
Private collection

Cat. 17
The Moorish Screen, 1921
Oil on canvas, 90.8 × 74.3 cm
Philadelphia Museum of Art, Philadelphia,
bequest of Lisa Norris Elkins, 1950

Cat. 18
Odalisque with a Screen, 1923
Oil on canvas, 61.5 × 50 cm
Statens Museum for Kunst, Copenhagen

Cat. 19
Interior: Flowers and Parakeets, 1924
Oil on canvas, 116.9 × 72.2 cm
The Baltimore Museum of Art, Baltimore, The Cone Collection,
formed by Dr Claribel Cone and Miss Etta Cone of Baltimore, Maryland
(BMA 1950.252)

Cat. 20
Young Woman Playing a Violin in Front of a Piano, *c.* 1924
Charcoal on paper, 31.2 × 47 cm
Collection Carol Selle

Cat. 21
Pianist and Still-life, 1924
Oil on canvas, 65 × 81.5 cm
Kunstmuseum, Berne

Cat. 22
Seated Odalisque, 1926
Oil on canvas, 73 × 60 cm
The Metropolitan Museum of Art, New York,
gift of Adele R. Levy Fund Inc., 1962 (62.112)

Cat. 23
Reclining Odalisque, 1926
Oil on canvas, 38.4 × 54.9 cm
The Metropolitan Museum of Art, New York,
bequest of Miss Adelaide Milton de Groot (1876–1967),
1967 (67.187.82)

Cat. 24
Seated Odalisque, Left Leg Bent, 1926
Oil on canvas, 65.4 × 46.1 cm
The Baltimore Museum of Art, Baltimore, The Cone Collection,
formed by Dr Claribel Cone and Miss Etta Cone of Baltimore, Maryland
(BMA 1950.251)

Cat. 25
Odalisque with Grey Culottes, 1926–27
Oil on canvas, 54 × 65 cm
Musée National de l'Orangerie, Paris

Cat. 26
**Decorative Figure on an
Ornamental Ground,** 1926
Oil on canvas, 130 × 98 cm
Musée National d'Art
Moderne, Centre Georges
Pompidou, Paris

Cat. 27
Reclining Odalisque, Green Culottes, Blue Belt, 1927
Oil on canvas, 50.8 × 60.96 cm
Private collection

Cat. 28
Odalisque with Grey Culottes, 1927
Oil on canvas, 64 × 81.3 cm
The Metropolitan Museum of Art, New York,
The Walter H. and Leonore Annenberg Collection,
gift of Walter H. and Leonore Annenberg, 1997,
bequest of Walter H. Annenberg, 2002 (1997.400)

Cat. 29
Two Odalisques, 1928
Oil on canvas, 54 × 65 cm
Moderna Museet, Stockholm

Cat. 30
Seated Odalisque, Left Knee Bent, Ornamental Background and Checkerboard, 1928
Oil on canvas, 55 × 37.8 cm
The Baltimore Museum of Art, Baltimore, The Cone Collection,
formed by Dr Claribel Cone and Miss Etta Cone of Baltimore, Maryland
(BMA 1950.255)

Cat. 31
Reclining Nude with Louis XIV Screen, 1923
Lithograph, 13 × 19 cm, on Chine paper, 28.7 × 37.6 cm
Victoria and Albert Museum, London

Cat. 32
Nude on a Divan with a Moucharabieh Background, 1922
Lithograph, 50 × 40.5 cm, on Chine paper, 59.7 × 44 cm
Victoria and Albert Museum, London

Cat. 33
Arabesque, 1924
Lithograph, 47.7 × 31.6 cm, on Chine paper, 59.4 × 43.2 cm
Victoria and Albert Museum, London

Cat. 34
Seated Odalisque with a Tulle Skirt, 1924
Lithograph, 36.7 × 27 cm, on Chine paper, 50.8 × 36.7 cm
Victoria and Albert Museum, London

Cat. 35
Standing Odalisque with a Tray of Fruit, 1924
Lithograph, 37.3 × 27.5 cm, on Japan paper, 48 × 33 cm
Victoria and Albert Museum, London

Cat. 36
Large Odalisque with Bayadère Costume, 1925
Lithograph, 54.2 × 44 cm, on Chine paper, 70.3 × 55.4 cm
Victoria and Albert Museum, London

Cat. 37
Odalisque with Red Satin Culottes, 1925
Lithograph, 18.7 × 26.7 cm, on Chine paper, 27.5 × 35.5 cm
Victoria and Albert Museum, London

Cat. 38
Odalisque with a Bowl of Fruit, 1925
Lithograph, 31.5 × 24.5 cm, on Chine paper, 47 × 32.5 cm
Victoria and Albert Museum, London

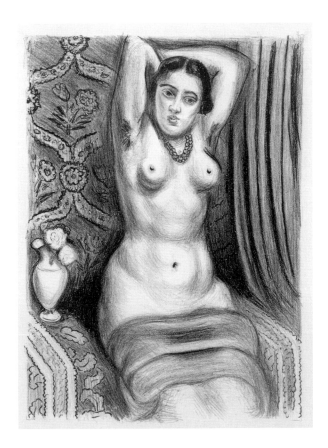

Cat. 39
Torso with Ewer, 1927
Lithograph, 37.7 × 26.5 cm, on Chine paper, 49.8 × 34.6 cm
Victoria and Albert Museum, London

Cat. 40
Odalisque, Samovar and Bowl of Fruit, 1929
Lithograph, 28 × 37.5 cm, on *vélin d'Arches*, 38.2 × 57 cm
Victoria and Albert Museum, London

Cat. 41
Reclining Nude with Bowl of Fruit, 1926
Lithograph, 43.6 × 54 cm, on Japan paper, 46.2 × 56 cm
Victoria and Albert Museum, London

Cat. 42
Reclining Nude, 1935
Pen and black ink on white paper, 37.7 × 55 cm
Mr and Mrs Thomas Gibson

Cat. 43
Purple Robe and Anemones, 1937
Oil on canvas, 73.1 × 60.5 cm
The Baltimore Museum of Art, Baltimore, The Cone Collection, formed by
Dr Claribel Cone and Miss Etta Cone of Baltimore, Maryland (BMA 1950.261)

Cat. 44
Small Odalisque in a Purple Robe, 1937
Oil on canvas, 38.1 × 45.7 cm
Private collection

Cat. 45
Odalisque with Yellow Persian Robe and Anemones, 1937
Oil on canvas, 73 × 60 cm
Philadelphia Museum of Art, Philadelphia,
The Samuel S. White 3rd and Vera White Collection, 1967

Cat. 46
Red Robe and Violet Tulips, 1937
Oil on canvas, 55 × 46 cm
Private collection

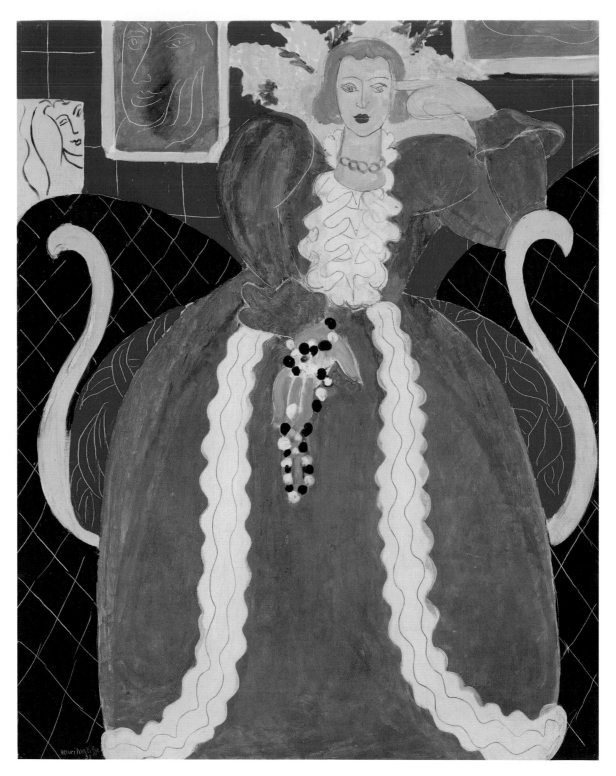

Cat. 47
Woman in Blue, 1937
Oil on canvas, 91 × 73 cm
Philadelphia Museum of Art, Philadelphia,
gift of Mrs John Wintersteen

Cat. 48
Seated Girl in Persian Robe, 1942
Oil on canvas, 43 × 56 cm
Musée Picasso, Paris

Cat. 49
Hélène au Cabochon, 1937
Oil on canvas, 55 × 33 cm
Private collection

Cat. 50
The Green Romanian Blouse, 1939
Oil on canvas, 61 × 46 cm
Private collection

Cat. 51
The Dream, 1940
Oil on canvas, 81 × 65 cm
Private collection

Cat. 52
The Lamé Robe, 1932
Pencil on paper, 32.4 × 25.4 cm
Yale University Art Gallery, New Haven, Connecticut,
gift of Stephen C. Clark

Cat. 53
The Romanian Blouse, c. 1936
Ink on paper, 38 × 28 cm
Pierre and Maria Gaetana Matisse Foundation Collection,
New York

Cat. 54
The Romanian Blouse, 1936
Pen and ink, 52.7 × 40.5 cm
The Pushkin State Museum of Fine Arts, Moscow

Cat. 55
Woman in an Embroidered Blouse with Necklace, 1936
Pen and ink on paper, 54 × 45 cm
Fogg Art Museum, Harvard University, Cambridge, Massachusetts,
bequest of Meta and Paul J. Sachs

Cat. 59
The Romanian Blouse, 1939
Ink on paper, 42 × 33 cm
Pierre and Maria Gaetana Matisse Foundation Collection, New York

Cat. 60
The Romanian Blouse, 1939
Charcoal on paper, 57 × 38.6 cm
Muzeul National de Artă al României, Bucharest

Cat. 61
Two Young Girls, Yellow Dress and Tartan Dress, 1941
Oil on canvas, 61 x 50 cm
Musée National d'Art Moderne, Centre Georges Pompidou, Paris,
on deposit at Musée départemental Matisse, Le Cateau-Cambrésis

Cat. 62
Woman in a White Coat, 1944
Oil on canvas, 72 × 60 cm
Private collection

Cat. 63
Woman in a Blue Gandoura, 1951
Oil on canvas, 81 × 65 cm
Musée départemental Matisse, Le Cateau-Cambrésis

Cat. 64
Themes and Variations
Series P, Woman Seated in an Armchair, pl. 1, 1942
Pen and ink, 50 × 40 cm approx.
Musée des Beaux-Arts, Lyons

Cat. 65
Themes and Variations
Series P, Woman Seated in an Armchair, pl. 2, 1942
Pen and ink, 50 × 40 cm approx.
Musée des Beaux-Arts, Lyons

Cat. 66
Themes and Variations
Series P, Woman Seated in an Armchair, pl. 3, 1942
Pen and ink, 50 × 40 cm approx.
Musée des Beaux-Arts, Lyons

Cat. 67
Themes and Variations
Series P, Woman Seated in an Armchair, pl. 4, 1942
Pen and ink, 50 × 40 cm approx.
Musée des Beaux-Arts, Lyons

Cat. 68
Themes and Variations
Series P, Woman Seated in an Armchair, pl. 5, 1942
Pen and ink, 50 × 40 cm approx.
Musée des Beaux-Arts, Lyons

Cat. 69
Themes and Variations
Series P, Woman Seated in an Armchair, pl. 6, 1942
Pen and ink, 50 × 40 cm approx.
Musée des Beaux-Arts, Lyons

The Colour of Ideas:
Chasubles and African Fabrics

Photographs of Matisse's bedroom taken by Henri Cartier-Bresson in 1944, in his Villa Le Rêve in Vence (fig. 60), show walls covered in Polynesian *tapas* and fragments of Kuba fabrics from Africa (pp. 157–59). These fabrics are made of natural fibres and are formed by the repetition of a geometric pattern over the whole surface; although the pattern is repeated, there are small variations in the design because the piece is hand woven. Matisse was challenged by the decorative appeal of these pieces.

He had just finished the plates for the book he was to entitle *Jazz*. In order to produce this important but small-scale work, he used a process that he had recently invented – he cut shapes from paper painted with gouache and fixed them on to a background. This was such a success that he began to wonder how these pure, free colours could be used for mural decorations of increasingly monumental size. The African and Polynesian fabrics began to lead him towards what he wanted: harmony between the decorative impact of the geometrical patterns and the expression of emotion that is the artist's prerogative, as he states, by 'simplifying' the means: 'Cut paper allows me to draw in

colour. For me, this is a simplification.... This simplification guarantees precision in the union of two materials which become one,' he explains. Matisse has colour at the ready, painted by his studio assistants on sheets of Canson paper. Instead of the lordly gesture of the brush inventing colour on the palette and on the canvas, and the line drawn irretrievably on the page, Matisse cuts out the shapes with scissors, building them up patiently by gradually adding one fragment after another, positioning them with the assistance of pins, and moving them painstakingly until he achieves the balance that he seeks.

The first two of his monumental cut-outs are the panels *Oceania: The Sky* and *Oceania: The Sea*, designed on the walls of his studio–bedroom; they bring back memories of the enchanting sea and sky of the lagoons of Oceania. The two *maquettes* were later stencilled on to linen to make mural hangings. The next monumental pieces were the *maquettes* for the stained-glass windows in the Dominican chapel at Vence, for which he cut 'live' into paper painted with green, yellow and blue gouache. The third version, a simple drawing of a leaf repeated in all the lancet

Opposite
Ngongo (sub-group of Kuba) cloth from
the Congo, late nineteenth or early twentieth
century
Embroidered raffia, 69 × 54 cm
Private collection

windows, echoes the monumental, soothing scale the building requires.

Shortly after this, he was required to design six large chasubles for the officiating clergy; he used immense sheets of paper like giant butterflies to create the semi-circular shape of the garments. He chose to cover the semicircles with a repeat pattern of simple forms, similar but different. He cut out flowers, fruit, butterflies, stars – to match the different seasons of the Catholic liturgy. Pink, red, green, yellow and white, purple, black: the chasubles represent the costumes for a sacred drama, solemn and stylised; the decorated fabrics have their own liturgical and transcendental part to play. DS

Opposite
Kuba cloth from the Congo, late nineteenth
or early twentieth century
Embroidered raffia, 75 × 36 cm
Private collection

Kuba-Shoowa cloth from the Congo,
late nineteenth or early twentieth century
Embroidered raffia, 86 × 19 cm
Private collection

Ngongo (sub-group of Kuba) cloth from the Congo,
late nineteenth or early twentieth century
Embroidered raffia, 138 × 54 cm
Private collection

Kuba-Shoowa cloth from the Congo, late nineteenth or early twentieth century
Embroidered raffia, 67 × 56 cm
Private collection

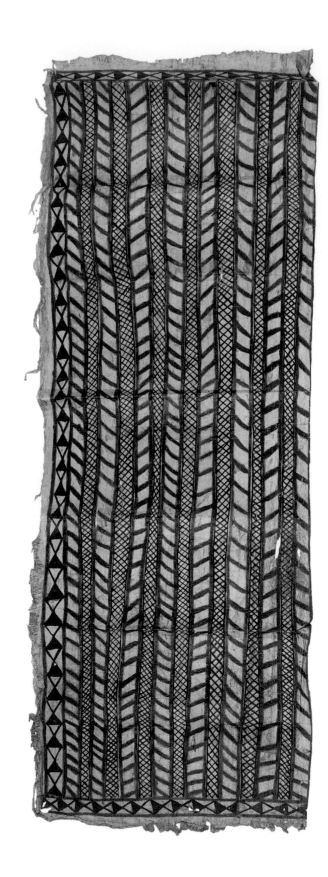

Tapa cloth (bark painting), n.d.
Pounded tree bark, 171 × 62 cm
Private collection

Polynesian tapa cloth (bark painting), n.d.
Pounded tree bark, 125 × 163 cm
Musée départemental Matisse, Le Cateau-Cambrésis,
gift of Marie Matisse, 1998
Formerly Henri Matisse Collection

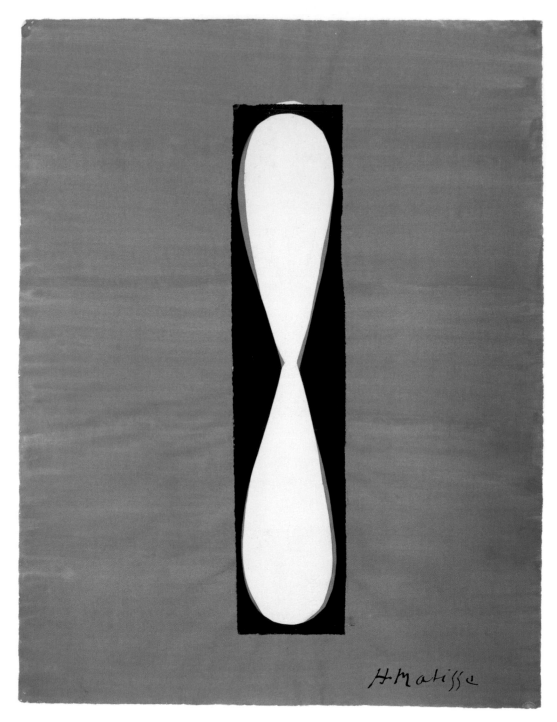

Cat. 70
Motif-L'hélice, 1945
Coloured gouache collage and ink on paper, 52.5 × 40.5 cm
Pierre and Maria Gaetana Matisse Foundation Collection, New York

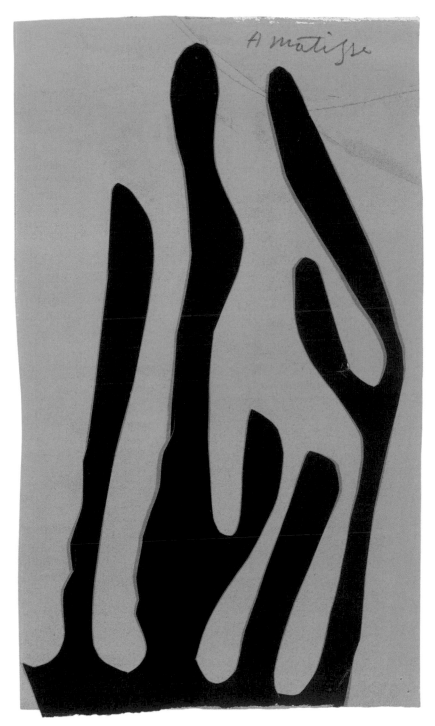

Cat. 71
Algae, 1947
Coloured gouache collage and ink on paper, 28.4 × 14.6 cm
Pierre and Maria Gaetana Matisse Foundation Collection, New York

Cat. 72
Black and Red Composition, 1947
Coloured gouache collage on paper, 40.6 × 52.7 cm
Davis Museum and Cultural Center, Wellesley College, Wellesley, MA,
gift of Professor and Mrs John McAndrew

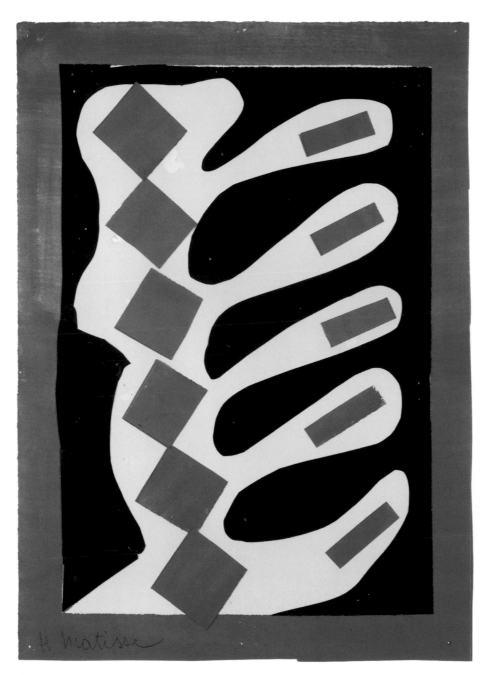

Cat. 73
Composition: Yellow, Blue and Black, 1947
Coloured gouache collage on paper, 47 × 34 cm
Thomas Gibson Fine Art Ltd

Cat. 74
Composition with a Red Cross, 1947
Coloured gouache collage on paper, 73 × 52.4 cm
Private collection, USA
Courtesy of Nancy Whyte Fine Arts, Inc., New York

Cat. 75
Negro Boxer, 1947
Coloured gouache collage on paper, 32 × 25.5 cm
Private collection
Courtesy of Yoshii Gallery, New York

Cat. 76
Four Rosettes with Blue Motifs, 1949–50
Gouache on cut paper pasted on paper support
and mounted on canvas, 36.9 × 53.4 cm
Private collection

Cat. 77
The Dancer, 1948
Coloured gouache on paper, cut and pasted to second sheet, 57.2 × 67.3 cm
Courtesy of The Metropolitan Museum of Art, New York. Lent by The Alex Hillman
Family Foundation

Cat. 78
Acrobatic Dancer, 1949
Coloured gouache collage and ink on paper, 52 × 40 cm
Pierre and Maria Gaetana Matisse Foundation Collection, New York

Cat. 79
Motif-feuille, c. 1950
Coloured gouache collage and ink on paper, 34 × 19.5 cm
Pierre and Maria Gaetana Matisse Foundation Collection, New York

Cat. 80
Snow Flowers, 1951
Watercolour and gouache on cut and pasted paper, 174 × 80.6 cm
The Metropolitan Museum of Art, New York, Jacques and Natasha Gelman
Collection, 1998 (1999.363.46)

Cat. 81
Black Leaf on a Green Ground, 1952
Coloured gouache collage on paper,
60 × 39 cm
The Menil Collection, Houston

Cat. 82
Costume for *Le Chant du rossignol*, 1919–20
Cotton and wool felt robe, appliquéd with blue-black silk velvet, 168 × 160 cm
Musée d'Art et d'Histoire, Geneva

Cat. 83
Black chasuble (front), 1950–52
Silk, 127 × 197 cm
Musée départemental Matisse,
Le Cateau-Cambrésis

Cat. 84
Black chasuble (back), 1950–52
Silk, 133 × 198 cm
Musée départemental Matisse,
Le Cateau-Cambrésis

Cat. 85
Maquette for the white chasuble,
1950–51
Coloured gouache collage on paper,
130 × 200 cm
Musée départemental Matisse,
Le Cateau-Cambrésis

Page 176, top left
A length of striped orange-and-green
silk, of uncertain origin, probably
nineteenth century
Silk, 129 × 130 cm
Private collection

Page 176, top right
North African robe, second half of the
nineteenth century, possibly made from
French imported silk
Silk, 130 × 154 cm
Private collection

Page 176, bottom left
Moroccan embroidered silk cap,
nineteenth or early twentieth century
Silk, 10 × 20 cm
Private collection

Page 176, bottom right
Ottoman or North African child's bolero,
second half of the nineteenth century
Wool, 36 × 30 cm
Private collection

Page 177, top left
Silk brocade panel, Japanese, nineteenth
century
Silk brocade, 188 × 89.5 cm
Private collection

Page 177, bottom left
Scarf, twentieth century
Cotton, 56 × 107 cm
Private collection

Page 177, right
Indian phulkari embroidery, Punjab,
late nineteenth century
Silk, 205 × 37.5 cm
Private collection

Page 178
Middle Eastern ikat, possibly Persian,
nineteenth century
Silk, 176 × 107 cm
Private collection

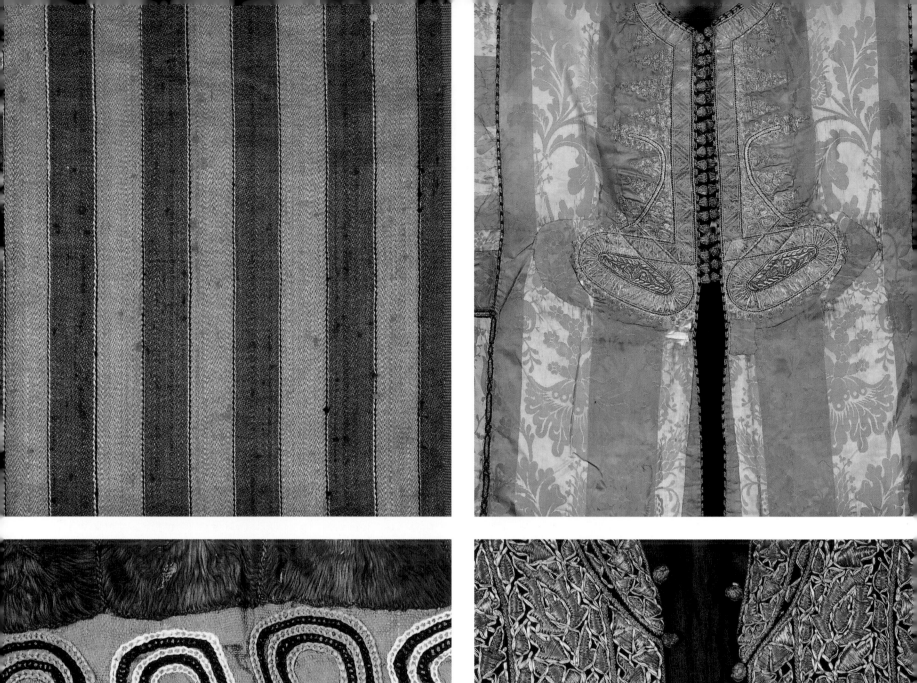

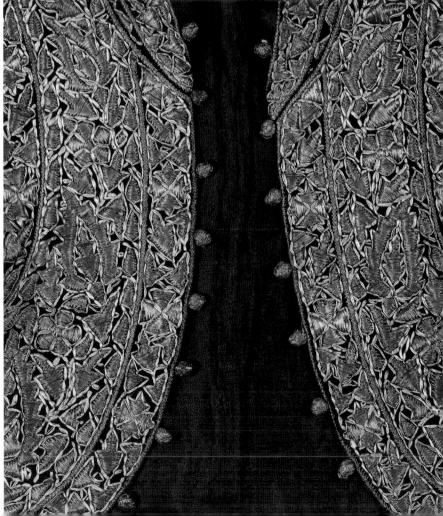

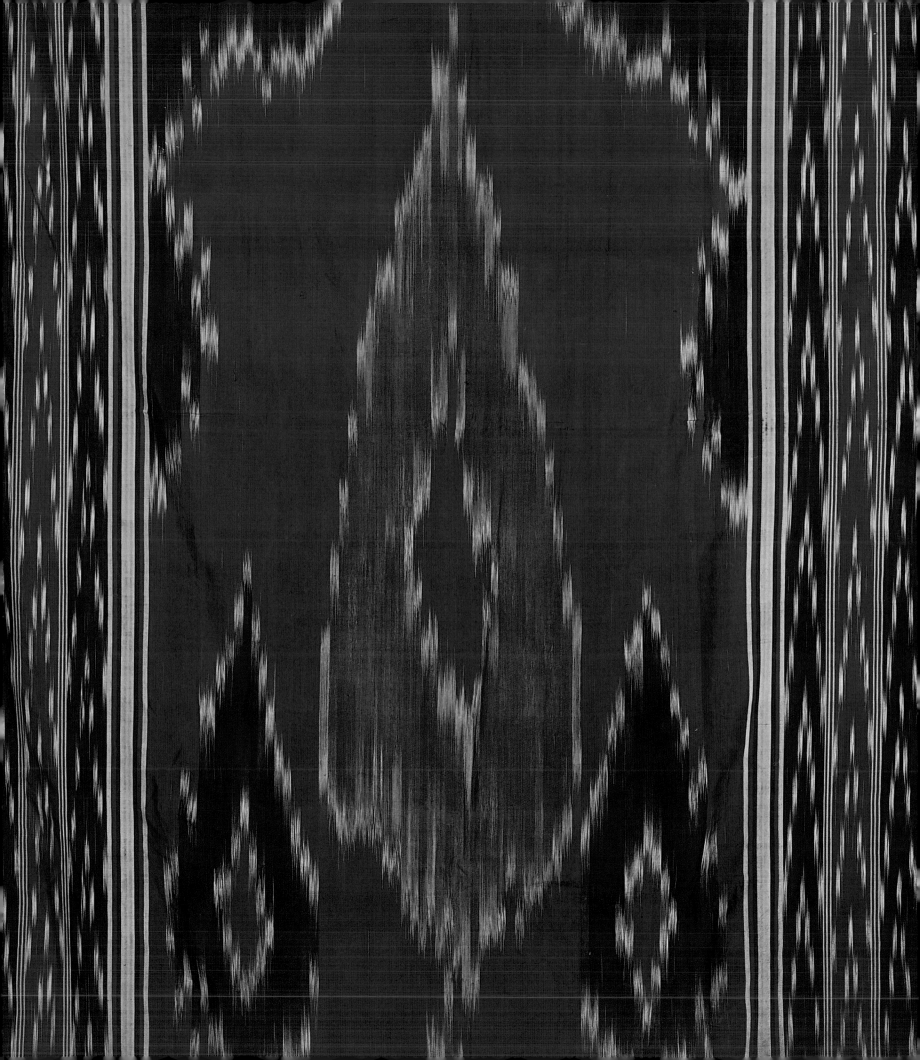

Catalogue entries

Cat. 1
Still-life, Books and Candle, 1890
Oil on canvas, 38.1 × 36 cm
Musée de Pontoise

'My second painting', as he subtitled it, was painted in June 1890, when Matisse was twenty and at the very outset of his career. It shows the artist tackling a conventional subject as an exercise in composition and technique. A pile of books, a guttering candle, a familiar *vanitas* symbol conveying the message of life's transience, placed on a table covered with an oriental carpet are staple components of Dutch seventeenth-century still-life painting. In this work they provide a neutral and static subject with which the apprentice painter could test his skills in depicting the play of light over a variety of textures and surfaces from the worn leather-book covers to the gleaming brass candlestick and the contrasts of light and dark established by the white matte newspaper and the black space beyond.

Matisse had recently discovered his artistic vocation while convalescing from a bout of pneumonia and had begun attending early morning classes at the local municipal art school, the Ecole Quentin de La Tour at St-Quentin, not far from his home town of Bohain, which also offered classes in tapestry and textile design. He also taught himself by studying Frédéric Goupil's *General and Complete Manual of Paintings in Oils*. *Still-life, Books and Candle* was probably copied from a chromolithograph, a standard practice at the time. Nevertheless, Matisse himself clearly considered this painting an accomplished achievement: for ten years after he had painted it, he claimed it contained everything he had done since, and, on seeing it after twenty years, he felt he had still made no further progress.[1] AD

1 Courthion A, p. 10, and Walter Pach, TS, note on Henri Matisse, 12 December 1953, Pierre Matisse Gallery Archives, Pierpont Morgan Library, New York, quoted in Spurling 1998, pp. 47 and 433, notes 70 and 71.

Cat. 2 (LC-C ONLY)
Still-life with Schiedam, 1896
Oil on canvas, 29 × 35 cm
Musée départemental Matisse, Le Cateau-Cambrésis

This still-life of 1896 depicts traditional objects that reflect light (glass, pewter), placed around various pieces of fruit that provide colour, on a white cloth. Matisse borrows his treatment of flat white areas from Manet, using them to define the different zones and paint them without modulations. The difficult problem of conveying the whiteness of a piece of fabric while preserving the sensation of thickness and rendering its drape recurs constantly in Flemish and Spanish painting. Thanks to its juxta-position with the black background, the white fabric becomes the main subject of the work. It captures the light and diffuses it to the objects. The absence of shading promises a new concept of space in this painting; shortly afterwards the Renaissance idea of perspective will be discarded. DS

Cat. 3 (LC-C/RA)
Bouquet of Daisies, c. 1895
Oil on canvas, 95 × 80 cm
Musée départemental Matisse, Le Cateau-Cambrésis

Throughout his life Matisse was always surrounded by flowers: bunches of daisies, anemones, tulips, jasmine, dog roses, lilies, sprays of magnolia, medlar ... and they became a favourite subject in his paintings and drawings.

Matisse was particularly sensitive to the light and shade in the Dutch paintings he copied in the Louvre. In this *Bouquet of Daisies* he heightens the dark tones with touches of light and the white of the flowers. The vase is placed on a table covered with a fabric whose colours merge into one another. This indefinable mix of tones contrasts with the clarity of the flowers standing in the light, which is also reflected by the mirror. The colours are dark and are dominated by green, brown ochre and red; the atmosphere is peaceful and harmonious, belonging to the classical tradition. Until his discovery

of the Impressionists in Brittany in 1896, and especially of the colour of the Corsican landscape, Matisse claimed not to be interested in anything but painting different greys and muted tones. DS

Cat. 4
The Breton Weaver, 1895–96
Oil on wood, 40 × 54.5 cm
Signed bottom right: H. Matisse
Musée National d'Art Moderne, Centre Georges Pompidou, Paris, on deposit at the Musée départemental Matisse, Le Cateau-Cambrésis

This painting of a weaver was begun in Brittany during the summer of 1895. Matisse visited the region over three consecutive summers in 1895, 1896 and 1897. In 1895 he travelled in the company of the painter Emile Wéry to the island of Belle-Ile-en-Mer off the rugged Atlantic coast before moving north to the little medieval town of St-Croix in Finistère and then on to the coastal village of Beuzec, where he found lodgings with a peasant family. Later Matisse recalled a cow eating hay in the corner of the room while its owner worked at his loom weaving the fabric for the family's clothes.[1] The subject would have had personal significance for Matisse, who had grown up among a community of textile weavers in Bohain-en-Vermandois in northern France, but he must have been struck by the difference between this Breton peasant's primitive loom and the much more sophisticated Jacquard looms which produced the very refined fabrics that had made Bohain's fortune.[2] Perhaps, too, he was aware of Van Gogh's powerful early paintings of weavers working at their looms.

The enormous contraption dominates the humble room with its rough, stone wall and bare floor painted in sombre greys, creams and neutral tones. This muted palette is typical of the empty landscapes, interiors and figure subjects that Matisse painted in the summers of 1895 and 1896 in Brittany and completed over the winters in his Paris studio. AD

1 See Spurling 1998, pp. 106 and 438, note 29.
2 Spurling 1998, p. 438.

Cat. 5
Pierre Matisse with Bidouille, 1904
Oil on canvas, 73.7 × 59 cm
Private collection

The small child in this painting is Pierre, Matisse's second son. He was four years old at the time and had recently recovered from a potentially life-threatening bout of bronchial pneumonia. Pierre stands in a room in his parents' tiny apartment on the quai St-Michel in the Latin Quarter of Paris. He is a poignant little figure, wan and frail, clutching a favourite wooden horse called Bidouille, and dwarfed by a large wooden armoire behind him. To his right is a painting by his father on an easel. The pictorial space is dominated by a table covered with a boldly patterned cloth, on which stands a potted plant still wrapped in the florist's paper. This painting is one of the first instances that the celebrated 'toile de Jouy'[1] appears in a work by Matisse. The cool blues of the cloth contrast with the warmer tones of the room and Pierre's red overall. The patterned cloth is depicted in a loose, vigorous style unconcerned with a precise rendering of the motif. Only a year or two later, in *Still-life with Blue Tablecloth* (cat. 7), this motif bursts beyond the confines of the tablecloth and signals a new departure in Matisse's art, when he would invent a different kind of pictorial space. AD

1 In fact, as noted in 'A Balance of Forces', the so-called toile de Jouy was not a real piece of toile de Jouy. It is probably a late nineteenth-century design and bears no relationship to the traditional toile de Jouy patterns that were produced at Jouy en Josas from 1760 to 1843.

Cat. 6 (RA/NY)
The Guitarist, 1903
Oil on canvas, 55 × 46 cm
Private collection, Switzerland
Courtesy of Pierre Sebastien Fine Art

The Guitarist is one of several paintings of this subject that Matisse painted in 1903, including one for which his wife posed in Spanish costume (Private collection) and another showing a seated male guitarist (Private collection). From 1900 to 1903 Matisse had concentrated primarily on the human figure in paintings and sculptures. The paintings produced at this time display the modelling and richly textured painterly surfaces Matisse had learnt from the work of Manet and Cézanne. No doubt the Spanish subject of *The Guitarist* also alludes to Manet's many Spanish subjects. A few years later, the Spanish theme reappears with *Spanish Woman with a Tambourine* (1909; The Pushkin State Museum of Fine Arts, Moscow), the two Spanish still-lifes (both winter of 1910–11; The State Hermitage Museum, St Petersburg; cat. 11 and fig. 36) and *The Manila Shawl* (1911; fig. 20), for which Mme Matisse was again the model. The group of guitarist pictures is probably the first to show Matisse's taste for the exotic and for dressing up, which emerged fully in the theatrical tableaux he created in his many odalisque paintings of the 1920s. In *The Guitarist* the 'toile de Jouy' makes only a modest appearance as a backdrop. AD

Cat. 7

Still-life with Blue Tablecloth, 1905–06
Oil on canvas, 73 × 92 cm
Signed bottom left: Henri Matisse
The State Hermitage Museum, St Petersburg, inv. 7696

In *Still-life with Blue Tablecloth*, the familiar piece of blue 'toile de Jouy' is no longer a simple decorative backdrop as in *The Guitarist* (1903; cat. 6), but now becomes the galvanising force of the whole composition, simultaneously anchoring and destabilising the still-life objects and filling the canvas with its energy and colour. The flower baskets and garlands of the traditional French textile design explode in splashes of white, mauve and blue. Purple-blue streaks crackle across the tablecloth, bursting beyond its edges, and hover above the fruit bowl before shooting up the wall behind. Spattered dabs of orange, yellow and blue, quieter residues of these pyrotechnics, enliven the neutral background. The play of hot reds and yellows against cooler blues suggests not

only Matisse's debt to Cézanne, but also the unprecedented intensity of colour in his own Fauve pictures of 1905. The spectral presence of another of Matisse's favourite textiles, the North African mat[1] that appears in other still-lifes of the same period (cat. 8), is apparent in the broken yellow line that defines its rectangular shape. AD

1 The design of this prayer-mat is typical of a place called Haouz on the plain of Marakesh, Morocco.

Cat. 8 (RA/NY)

Dishes and Fruit on a red-and-black Rug, 1906
Oil on canvas, 61 × 73 cm
Signed bottom left: Henri Matisse
Inscribed on the reverse of the picture: 1906, Salon d'Automne
The State Hermitage Museum, St Petersburg, inv. 8998

In May 1906 Matisse visited Algeria and brought back from Biskra some crockery and textiles that he depicted in several works. *Dishes and Fruit on a red-and-black Rug* marks a transition in Matisse's work from his Fauvist style of 1905, when he first pushed colours to their maximum chromatic intensity, to his next phase, when he explored the decorative possibilities of colour and flatness. The red rug dominates the painting, filling most of the pictorial field. A glass vessel retains its three-dimensional integrity, but the other still-life fruits and objects are only summarily described and seem more or less absorbed into the decorative patterning of the rug. Matisse further explored the dramatic potential of this North African fabric in *Still-life with a Red Rug* (1906; Musée de Grenoble). AD

Cat. 9 (RA/NY)

Still-life with Blue Tablecloth, 1909
Oil on canvas, 88 × 118 cm
The State Hermitage Museum, St Petersburg, inv. 6569

A few years after painting *Still-life with Blue Tablecloth* (1905–06; cat. 7), Matisse began creating his boldest textile

painting to date, taking inspiration from the 'toile de Jouy' cloth. In *Still-life with Blue Tablecloth* the baskets of flowers encircled by garlands burst out of the traditional textile design to fill virtually the entire canvas with their sweeping blue arabesques. The coffee-pot, green flask and compotier of apples, as well as the patterned background and pervasive blue, are all familiar from Cézanne, Matisse's lifelong mentor, but now the still-life objects are reduced to mere tokens precariously afloat on the billowing blue fabric that subverts conventional notions of perspective. Only a discreet wedge of space at the far right breaks the illusion of assertive flatness. Matisse's investigations of the tension between flatness and depth were paralleled at this time by Picasso's and Braque's very different and more muted fragmenting of forms and space in their immediately pre-Cubist paintings. AD

Cat. 10 (RA ONLY)

Portrait of Greta Moll, 1908
Oil on canvas, 93 × 73.4 cm
Signed and dated lower left: Henri Matisse, 1908
The Trustees of The National Gallery, London

Greta Moll was a German painter and sculptress who, aged twenty-four, was the youngest pupil at the painting class (later known as the Académie Matisse) that Matisse started in 1907 in the Couvent des Oiseaux, an old convent in rue de Sèvres, Paris. She and her husband, the painter Oskar Moll, were early collectors of Matisse's work. Matisse has painted a powerful portrait of the striking young woman whose golden hair and blue eyes made him think of 'honey and ripe corn'.[1] The backdrop is the familiar piece of blue-and-white 'toile de Jouy' that Matisse had used with such startling effect in his great still-lifes *Harmony in Red* (1908; fig. 2) and *Still-life with Blue Tablecloth* (1909; cat. 9). In this portrait the bold blue arabesques cleverly echo the striking curves of Greta's rounded face and heavy arms. This juxtaposition of the calm, statuesque figure with a patterned textile inevitably brings to mind female portraits by Ingres, whom Matisse

admired. Matisse himself recalled how he had drastically simplified his original concept of his portrait after studying Veronese's *La Bella Nani* (1560) in the Louvre. However, Greta and Oskar Moll were 'completely devastated by the results of my work, which struck them as disastrous'.[2] Yet they altered their opinion of the portrait and fifty years later Greta noted: 'The painting became ours, and we loved it more and more. It is one of Matisse's most beautiful and powerful works.'[3] AD

1 Statement by Henri Matisse on Oskar and Greta Moll, Matisse Archives, Paris, quoted in Spurling 1998, pp. 410 and 463, note 150.
2 Quoted in Spurling 1998, p. 411.
3 Margarete Moll, 'Erinnerungen an Henri Matisse' in Kaiserslautern 1989, p. 45, quoted in Spurling 1998, pp. 411 and 427, note 154.

Cat. 11 (RA/NY)

Seville Still-life, 1910–11
Oil on canvas, 90 × 117 cm
Signed lower right: Henri Matisse
The State Hermitage Museum, St Petersburg, inv. 6570

Matisse spent the winter of 1910 to 1911 in Spain visiting Madrid, Cordoba, Granada and Seville, where he painted two still-lifes, *Seville Still-life* and the closely related *Spanish Still-life* (fig. 36), both in The State Hermitage Museum, St Petersburg. Matisse has piled up on a sofa some fabrics he had picked up in Spain. They are dominated by the coverlet from the Sierra Nevada he had bought in Madrid that will reappear in *The Pink Studio* (1911; cat. 12). Originally, as Matisse explained in a letter to his wife, this textile was white with blue motifs, but, in these two Spanish still-lifes, he transposes the colours to white or cream on blue.[1] The result is a riotous profusion of texture and colour that throbs and vibrates against a hot tangerine ground. Even the geranium growing in its pot is completely engulfed by the rampant jungle growth that crawls across the canvas. Matisse's exposure to Muslim art in the architecture of Andalusia he saw in Spain, during his travels in North Africa and, above all, at the great exhibition of Islamic art in Munich in 1910, had taught him a whole new visual vocabulary that liberated his innate sense of the abstract and decorative. AD

1 Letter of 11 December 1910 to Amélie Matisse. Matisse Archives, Paris.

Cat. 12
The Pink Studio, 1911
Oil on canvas, 179.5 × 221 cm
The Pushkin State Museum of Fine Arts, Moscow

A soft radiant light bathes the artist's large and airy studio, tingeing the walls in a lilac pink that deepens to coral as it floods across the floor. The Pink Studio is the first of the four majestic interiors that Matisse painted in 1911, along with Interior with Aubergines (fig. 25), The Red Studio (fig. 13) and The Painter's Family (fig. 11), each on the same grand scale and each unified by an all-embracing colour or a pervasive plethora of pattern, which simultaneously suppresses and amplifies space. The uplifting serenity of this interior belies its conceptual and spatial complexity. The large yellow rug to the left leads the viewer rapidly into the deep space of the picture, but the different perspectives that Matisse employs in other parts of the composition, notably the plunging view down onto the stool on the far right, veer in different directions. Matisse had been profoundly affected by the Persian miniatures he had seen in the great exhibition of Islamic art in Munich in 1910, which, with their cellular organisation, had suggested new ways of organising pictorial space. Arranged along the back wall are paintings and sculptures that constitute a sort of review of Matisse's own work from 1906 to 1911. Prominent among them are, to the left, the sculpture Decorative Figure (1908; Hirshhorn Museum and Sculpture Garden, Smithsonian Institution, Washington DC), on the wall above Le Luxe (II) (1907; Statens Museum for Kunst, Copenhagen), and just visible on the extreme right is the edge of Dance (I)

(1909; Museum of Modern Art, New York). Significantly, however, the centre of the composition is dominated not by a painting, but by a piece of decorative fabric, the coverlet from the Sierra Nevada that Matisse, reversing its original colour scheme, decorated with cream motifs on a deep-blue ground. Its vigorous plant forms, augmented by the little sprigs of pink flowers on the wings of the screen, suggest a metaphor for growth and creativity. AD

Cat. 13 (LC-C ONLY)
Study for **Basket of Oranges**, 1912
Pen and ink, 26 × 17.1 cm
Signed in the centre: Tanger, H. Matisse
Musée Picasso, Paris

This study for the Basket of Oranges was painted in Tangier at the beginning of 1912; it is a small drawing in pen and ink and shows the flowered pattern on the tablecloth much more clearly than the basket of oranges, which is only roughly sketched in. 'The basket rests on a table covered with a white silk cloth with large bunches of blue [and] yellow and green flowers,'[1] Matisse wrote to Michael Stein about the painting he was just finishing.[2] The drawing is characteristic of Matisse's use of decorative pattern. Each element of the design is personalised by its difference from all the other elements. Matisse has altered the embroidered bunches of flowers until they have become the true subject of the drawing. DS

1 See Hilary Spurling, 'Material World: Matisse, His Art and His Textiles', note 7.
2 Henri Matisse 1904–1917, exh. cat., Musée National d'Art Moderne, Centre Georges Pompidou, Paris, 1993, p. 484.

Cat. 14
Corner of the Artist's Studio, 1912
Oil on canvas, 191.5 × 114 cm
The Pushkin State Museum of Fine Arts, Moscow

In Corner of the Artist's Studio Matisse zooms in on the Spanish coverlet and floral screen, familiar from The Pink Studio (1911; cat. 12), but the diminutive,

empty, green vase in that painting has now grown into a monumental two-handled amphora supporting a red-and-yellow flowerpot, from which springs a flourishing plant. There is a reminder of the pot of nasturtiums in Nasturtiums with 'Dance' (I) (1912; Metropolitan Museum of Art, New York) and Nasturtiums with 'Dance' (II) (1912; The Pushkin State Museum of Fine Arts, Moscow). Its leafy tendrils pick up the dancing rhythm of the textile motifs, reinforcing the sense of vital fecundity. The subject is Matisse's studio at Issy-les-Moulineaux in the suburbs of Paris. A gaily striped red-and-yellow deckchair occupies the left of the composition, echoing the colours of the flowerpot. Matisse now changes the floor from orange pink to a dense emerald green, thereby giving each section of the composition an equal visual weight and intensifying the chromatic register throughout. Corner of the Artist's Studio was commissioned by the Russian textile merchant Sergei Shchukin, one of Matisse's main patrons. It is possible that it was intended as a pendant to Nasturtiums with 'Dance' (I), as both canvases are the same size and were acquired by Shchukin.[1] AD

1 Barr 1975, p. 157.

Cat. 15
Plaster Figure with Bouquet of Flowers, 1919
Oil on canvas, 113 × 87 cm
Museu de Arte de São Paolo Assis Chateaubriand, São Paolo
Formerly Leigh B. Block Collection

Plaster Figure with Bouquet of Flowers is one of several large-scale still-lifes painted at Issy-les-Moulineaux near Paris in the summer of 1919. That summer marked the end of a period of transition in Matisse's painting vocabulary, leading to his 'Nice' style of female figures in a decorative setting during the 1920s. In Plaster Figure with Bouquet of Flowers the elements of figure and decoration are evident. The previous year Matisse had been working on sculpture at the Ecole des Arts Décoratifs, where he had

explored the construction of classical sculpture, such as the Hellenistic Crouching Venus, the impetus for the very animated plaster figure here.[1] A plaster figure is placed on a prosaic wooden table, along with a bouquet of flowers against a background of the familiar 'toile de Jouy'. In Plaster Figure with Bouquet of Flowers Matisse enlarges a single element of the 'toile de Jouy', emphasising the white background of the fabric, which he depicts as a swirling, turbulent river of plaster-like, blue-tinged paint, similar to the surface of the plaster figure. Figure and fabric are made complementary.

To the dialogue between sculptural volume and two-dimensional painting, represented by the painting of the kneeling classical figure on the wall, can be added the decorative, elevated to the status of 'high art'. KB

1 Schneider 1984, p. 536.

Cat. 16
Pansies, 1918–19
Oil on paper mounted on wood, 48.9 × 45.1 cm
The Metropolitan Museum of Art, New York, bequest of Joan Whitney Payson, 1975 (1976.201.22)

In this strikingly unconventional still-life, Matisse explores the dynamic spatial relationship between a small glass vase of pansies resting precariously near the edge of a table whose corner thrusts boldly into the flat decorative backdrop provided by the now familiar 'toile de Jouy'. Not for the first time Matisse permits an actual living flower or plant to be utterly overwhelmed by the sheer vigour of the printed flora motifs in the fabric that had provided the inspiration for some of his most daring compositions for over a decade. We can observe a similar relationship in Still-life with Blue Tablecloth (cat. 9) and also in Seville Still-life (cat. 11), in which the untrammelled, fecund motifs in an assortment of patterned textiles assert the key role they played in Matisse's pictorial vision.

Pansies bears a close relationship to the larger Plaster Figure with a Bouquet of Flowers (cat. 15), painted around the same time in the studio at Issy-les-Moulineaux. Both works mark the end of a phase in Matisse's art in which he explored the visual tensions between textile background and foreground props, before moving on, in the 1920s, to the densely patterned artifice of the Nice interiors with odalisques. However, whereas in *Plaster Figure with a Bouquet of Flowers* the monumental classical figure asserts its presence against the 'toile de Jouy', in *Pansies* the fragility of the tiny flowers serves only to emphasise the sheer force of the textile, while the uncompromising tabletop holds the picture in balance. AD

Cat. 17

The Moorish Screen, 1921
Oil on canvas, 90.8 × 74.3 cm
Philadelphia Museum of Art, Philadelphia, bequest of Lisa Norris Elkins, 1950

Matisse painted *The Moorish Screen* shortly after he moved to his new studio and apartment at place Charles-Félix in Nice in the autumn of 1921. The two fashionably dressed young women in the painting are depicted in one of the apartment's two large rooms. A Moorish screen dominates the interior, creating a division between the sitting-room and the bedroom behind it. A violin case is visible on the bed. In the sitting-room one woman leans casually on the mantelpiece, while the other sits at a pedestal table with an open book beside her. A contemporary photograph by Man Ray shows Matisse painting his model Henriette Darricarrère, who is reading at a table in this room, with the lattice-patterned Moorish screen, or *moucharabieh*, partly visible behind her, as well as the floral wallpaper.

In the painting the two sketchy white figures stand out against the large blocks of floral patterning – the blue oriental runner, the red floral carpet, as well as the screen and wallpaper – transforming the bourgeois interior into an abstract space. The aerial perspective gives a sense of compressed, airless space, while the whiteness of the dresses and the light areas of the screen and carpets lend the interior a luminous quality. KB

Cat. 18 (LC-C/RA)

Odalisque with a Screen, 1923
Oil on canvas, 61.5 × 50 cm
Statens Museum for Kunst, Copenhagen

Odalisque with a Screen, one of a number of paintings on the subject from the mid-1920s, portrays the model Henriette Darricarrère posing semi-nude in striped harem pants, with her arms raised like an oriental dancer. The painting features a number of decorative elements that form a patterned backdrop to the costumed figure: the folding screen and the *moucharabieh*, a large decorative panel covered with fabric. These props figure in photographs of Matisse's studio taken during the 1920s in his apartment in place Charles-Félix, Nice. Cushions, tambourines, vases and plants furnish the exotic stage-sets in which the artist painted the model.

The deceptively easy aesthetic of Matisse's Nice period belies the careful construction of the painting – a play on two- and three-dimensional space. Set at an angle, the screen, with its smudged lavender 1920s-style floral motif, cuts across the schematic architectural lines of the *moucharabieh*, which depicts an Islamic façade and arch suggesting depth. The curved greenish-yellow stripes of the model's costume and the rigid vertical leaves of the plant organise the broad areas of pale, washed colour into verticals and horizontals. The alluring female figure also appears as one more decorative ornament, albeit the central one. KB

Cat. 19 (NY ONLY)

Interior: Flowers and Parakeets, 1924
Oil on canvas, 116.9 × 72.2 cm
The Baltimore Museum of Art, Baltimore, The Cone Collection, formed by Dr Claribel Cone and Miss Etta Cone of Baltimore, Maryland (BMA 1950.252)

Interior: Flowers and Parakeets depicts the two front studio rooms of Matisse's place Charles-Félix apartment with its rich, oriental décor and window overlooking Nice, the sea and the Mediterranean sky. The narrow vertical focus, distorted by the elevated viewpoint, directs the

spectator's view to the window, visible through the drapery, which is drawn to one side. Along this trajectory are areas of clashing patterns: the yellow and red 1920s orientalist fabric draped over the table contrasts with the red and pink floral carpet and the lavender Rococo-style fabric of the folding screen. The still-life on the table, the vase of yellow flowers and the birdcage, impressionistically painted, contribute to the complexity of the scheme.

In the upper left-hand corner Matisse depicts overlapping floral fabrics that include the *moucharabieh*, with its cut-out Islamic arch. The dark shadow on the extreme left, and the almost anthropomorphic black area outlined by the keyhole arch, create an air of mystery. (In the pair to this work, *Interior with a Phonograph* of 1924 in a private collection, Matisse portrays his own reflection in this space.) The almost cinematic sense of convergence towards deep space deceives the eye to experience three-dimensional space in what is no more than a two-dimensional design. KB

Cat. 20 (RA/NY)

Young Woman Playing a Violin in Front of a Piano, c. 1924
Charcoal on paper, 31.2 × 47 cm
Collection Carol Selle

The charcoal drawing *Young Woman Playing a Violin in Front of a Piano* seems a realistic work, removed from the usual oriental trappings and colour of the Nice studio. The model is depicted naturalistically in tonal greys and black, and her features are clearly legible. Her black dress has a white neckline and cuffs. The young woman, the model Henriette Darricarrère, did, in fact, play the violin and the piano. Matisse also played the violin, and so the instrument provides an autobiographical reference, as well as an allusion to the associated activities of art and music.

In the background, the recognisable floral-patterned screen, or *moucharabieh*, contrasts with the geometric construction of the subject. The perpendicular line of the bow, the right angle of the violinist's arm, the black-and-white

verticals of the piano keys and the rectangular pages of music create a linear pattern, tilted slightly to the left and seen from a raised viewpoint. The geometric construction of the figure and instruments works against the patterned screen, which has strong vertical lines and arched panels, creating a play between real and abstract space, and between the structured world of music and the sensual realm of art. KB

Cat. 21 (RA ONLY)

Pianist and Still-life, 1924
Oil on canvas, 65 × 81.5 cm
Kunstmuseum, Berne

Pianist and Still-life is one of a group of paintings depicting the theme of music, in which Henriette Darricarrère plays an instrument in a domestic interior. The related pursuits of art and music were part of Henriette's real life, as they were for Matisse and his family. In this painting Henriette plays an upright piano in a dark interior. The soft earth tones of the furnishings – the dark-grained wood of the piano, the heavy brown curtain, the ochre-coloured table, the muted reds of the floor and upholstery – suggest an air of quiet reflection. The dark-haired pianist is dressed in black, an important part of the colour orchestration as Matisse describes it, 'comparable to that of the double-bass as a solo instrument'.[1]

In the background the North African hanging provides the only light source, suggesting yet another dimension in this otherwise sombre atmosphere. In the foreground the still-life comprises a large pineapple in a ceramic bowl, a glass vase of flowers, scattered pieces of fruit, and a floral ceramic vase, displayed on a large metal tray. *Pianist and Still-life* combines the world of the senses, referring to the classical theme of still-life, as well as the intellectual realm of music and art. KB

1 'Black is a Colour', 1946, trans. in Flam 1995, p. 107.

Cat. 22

Seated Odalisque, 1926
Oil on canvas, 73 × 60 cm
The Metropolitan Museum of Art, New York,
gift of Adele R. Levy Fund Inc., 1962 (62.112)

Seated Odalisque and Seated Odalisque, Left
Leg Bent (cat. 24) depict a real woman of
the time, fashionably dressed and sitting
on a black-and-yellow-striped chair,
looking out at the viewer with a serene
expression. Matisse often conceived his
paintings as pairs, as the similar
odalisque compositions, one viewed in
close-up, the other at a distance, indicate.
The odalisque wears green harem pants
with a red belt and a sheer blouse with
yellow embroidery. The provocatively
transparent blouse of the Metropolitan
Seated Odalisque reveals her rouged
nipples, implying modern sexuality
rather than oriental mystique. The pose
of the model Zita in Seated Odalisque,
Left Leg Bent is more modest. She is seen
from a distance and turned to the left,
obscuring her breasts with her right arm
as she leans forward in the chair.

In the background of both paintings
is the familiar latticework screen, or
moucharabieh, its pierced openings
coloured red and black. This pattern is
repeated in the red and black squares of
the lozenge-shaped floor tiles, which
meet the lattice screen at an angle. The
screen's curved arches reflect the
contours of the chair, the vertical stripes
of which run contrary to the lattice
design. At the same time, the arches
imply recession, while the pale-skinned
model of Seated Odalisque, who occupies
a disproportionately large space, is
projected forward. In close-up the details
of the screen are visible – the white
design around the arches and the
outlines of the lattice. The face of
the model is very legible, while the
background is somewhat distorted.
The model is real, but her surroundings
are ornamental. The observer's point of
view shifts between figure and ground,
between the two and the three-
dimensional. The repetition of the
lattice, constrained only by the borders
of the canvas, as well as the planes of
patterning, emphasises the decorative.
Seated Odalisque, Left Leg Bent may be

the complementary pair, but the effect of
the full body pose seen from an elevated
position could not be more different. In
this painting the odalisque is distorted,
her face more mask-like and the detail
of her costume not evident. The lattice
background and the lozenge floor tiles,
too, have no detail and are therefore
abstract. The incline of the floor appears
steeper due to the raised viewpoint.
The wide angle allows the observer to see
a black drapery with a schematic floral
design on the left-hand side closing
off the space. Matisse manipulates the
design elements, the colours and the
model's pose, which at first view seem
quite similar, to create different moods.
KB

Cat. 23

Reclining Odalisque, 1926
Oil on canvas, 38.4 × 54.9 cm
The Metropolitan Museum of Art, New York,
bequest of Miss Adelaide Milton de Groot
(1876–1967), 1967 (67.187.82)

In Reclining Odalisque Matisse places the
semi-nude model in a languorous pose,
lying on a divan with her arms behind
her head, with a samovar and Rococo
table to one side. The odalisque becomes
more sensuous in this painting and the
depiction of her and her environment
more complex. Matisse conveys the
receding levels of the fantasised studio
space he created by overloading the
painting with pattern and colour. It is
interesting to compare the painting to
contemporary photographs of the studio.
Behind the model there is a screen of
fabric with a stylised North African
design and, beyond, one of the familiar
Moroccan hangings.

In the painting the patterned
background suggests the floral wallpaper
and the floral hanging, partly visible,
and the narrow black area on the extreme
right could indicate the darkened
doorway. Speaking of his odalisque
paintings, inspired by the actual
hangings, rugs and costumes, Matisse
refers to an underlying pictorial tension
in the interrelationship of the elements
of the works, an indication of the
painter's own sublimated eroticism. KB

Cat. 24 (NY ONLY)

Seated Odalisque, Left Leg Bent, 1926
Oil on canvas, 65.4 × 46.1 cm
The Baltimore Museum of Art, Baltimore,
The Cone Collection, formed by Dr Claribel
Cone and Miss Etta Cone of Baltimore,
Maryland (BMA 1950.251)

See cat. 22

Cat. 25

Odalisque with Grey Culottes, 1926–27
Oil on canvas, 54 × 65 cm
Musée National de l'Orangerie, Paris

Matisse completes the paintings entitled
Odalisque with Grey Culottes in the spring
of 1927, two of a group of odalisques of
the later 1920s influenced by his turn to
sculpture. These paintings, inspired by
the sculpture Large Seated Nude (started
1925) and the painting Decorative Figure
on an Ornamental Ground (1926; cat. 26),
display a more solid and clear
construction. Both paintings emphasise
the stage-like setting in which the model
is posed, variously in the foreground
or in the recess. The pale, Ingresque
odalisque reclines in a relaxed,
horizontal position, arms at her side,
hands clasped and knees drawn up. She
wears grey culottes with a green belt that
correspond to the colours of the striped
bed. The samovar and Rococo table, the
only realistic objects, as well as the figure,
are set against layers of decorative
patterning: the terracotta and pale-green
floral wallpaper; the blue, yellow and
terracotta wide striped hanging; and the
yellow and pale-green drapery, drawn to
one side. The black and grey lattice-
patterned moucharabieh, of which only
a narrow section is visible, mirrors the
colour of the model's culottes and the
triangular shape of her pubis. The
excessive coloured patterning in this
pale, almost abstract work dominates the
odalisque in her sombre costume.

The red Odalisque with Grey Culottes
(cat. 28) bears a strong similarity to the
lithograph Odalisque, Samovar and Bowl
of Fruit (1929; cat. 40), in terms of its
construction and its features – the
overlapping floral hanging, the lattice-
design moucharabieh and red-, yellow-

and black-striped curtain, the pose
of the model and the props. The rich
reds, terracotta colours and the loose
brushwork of the second painting,
as well as its figures, provide a sharp
contrast with the paler tones of its calm-
inducing pair. The model in the red
Odalisque, inspired by Michelangelo's
figure Night on the Medici tomb,
contorts her muscular, terracotta torso,
as she leans on her left arm. Matisse's two
versions of Odalisque with Grey Culottes,
although similar in construction, could
not be more different in feeling. One
is derived from the 'classical' French
tradition, the other a Baroque-style
'Italianate' treatment of staccato rhythms
and dark colour. Yet in both paintings
the décor overwhelms the figure and
claims the spectator's attention more
than the model herself. KB

Cat. 26 (RA ONLY)

**Decorative Figure on an Ornamental
Ground**, 1926
Oil on canvas, 130 × 98 cm
Musée National d'Art Moderne, Centre Georges
Pompidou, Paris

Decorative Figure on an Ornamental
Ground, considered one of Matisse's most
significant works, is a bold experiment in
the relationship between figure and
ground. The seated nude, resembling an
important sculpture created by Matisse
at the time, Large Seated Nude (1925–29),
appears detached from the background,
which is composed of six different
ornamental patterns. On the wall, the
brown-and-blue outsized floral design
is repeated in the frame of the centrally
positioned Rococo-style mirror hung
in the middle. Running diagonal to the
background, stylised floral motifs and
the edge of the striped mat cover the
foreground. The blue-and-white Chinese
ceramic plant pot on the left, the bowl
of lemons in the centre foreground and
the floral square in the lower right-hand
corner – possibly a cushion or the back
of a chair – add to the surfeit of pattern.
Viewed as a flat, unified space, the
contrasting designs of the wall and floor
create an unsettling effect. The female
figure introduces volume into the

structure of the work, but remains an integral part of the ornamental whole. In Decorative Figure on an Ornamental Ground Matisse uses the decorative and the ornamental to structure the work, as he works towards a more simplified painting constructed with colour. KB

Cat. 27
Reclining Odalisque, Green Culottes, Blue Belt, 1927
Oil on canvas, 50.8 × 60.96 cm
Private collection

In Reclining Odalisque, Green Culottes, Blue Belt Matisse explores the theme of the odalisque, ornamentation and eroticism. The floral hanging, the moucharabieh and the drapery, as well as the parallel vertical stripes of the carpet, recall Matisse's familiar stage-set for the odalisque, which includes the samovar and Rococo table. The bare-breasted model, wearing floral-patterned green culottes and blue belt, reclines on a striped divan, a samovar and a Rococo table to one side. These objects and the odalisque herself stand out against the competing decorative patterns. The only areas without any pattern are the dark folds of drapery, which represent a studio doorway, and the model's torso and lower legs. Her sinuous, stretched-out body is traced with curved lines, repeated in the partly visible arch of the moucharabieh and the outline of the Rococo table and the samovar. These elements contrast with the strong verticals of the carpet and the lattice and floral design of the backdrop that provide the 'architecture' of the painting, as Matisse refers to it, which conveys a greater sense of eroticism than the female figure herself. KB

Cat. 28 (NY ONLY)
Odalisque with Grey Culottes, 1927
Oil on canvas, 64 × 81.3 cm
The Metropolitan Museum of Art, New York, The Walter H. and Leonore Annenberg Collection, gift of Walter H. and Leonore Annenberg, 1997, bequest of Walter H. Annenberg, 2002 (1997.400)

See cat. 25

Cat. 29 (RA ONLY)
Two Odalisques, 1928
Oil on canvas, 54 × 65 cm
Moderna Museet, Stockholm

The Two Odalisques of 1928 belongs to the final series of this subject. To the theme of the odalisque in an ornamental setting Matisse adds the sculptural nude, recalling his often-copied figure of Michelangelo's Night from the Medici tomb. The heavy, full-bodied Michelangelesque nude reclines on a solid green divan, propped on a cushion. Her mirror image, the reclining odalisque dressed in a harem costume, identical to the model in Odalisque with a Turkish Chair (1928; Musée d'Art Moderne de la Ville de Paris), twists her body, leg drawn up and left arm behind her head, in a sculptural pose. The pair, set against exaggeratedly Baroque wallpaper, reiterates the figure and background of Decorative Figure on an Ornamental Ground (1926; cat. 26).
    The horizontal figures appear to be clumsily placed against the various areas of patterning: the dark-red and black floral wall and blue polka-dot curtain with a bright yellow swag of fabric, the dark-black, red-and-blue paisley pattern of the fabric in the foreground. Matisse approaches the end of his treatment of figure and ornamental ground in this work that unites his experiments in painting and sculpture. KB

Cat. 30 (NY ONLY)
Seated Odalisque, Left Knee Bent, Ornamental Background and Checkerboard, 1928
Oil on canvas, 55 × 37.8 cm
The Baltimore Museum of Art, Baltimore, The Cone Collection, formed by Dr Claribel Cone and Miss Etta Cone of Baltimore, Maryland (BMA 1950.255)

Seated Odalisque, Left Knee Bent, Ornamental Background and Checkerboard, places the model in an upright position to fit within the narrow, elongated format. The raised perspective, allowing for a wide view of the studio stage-set, distorts the space, making the model's position ambiguous. The dark, rich tones

– the red and pink of the floral and lattice foreground, the dark pink of the model's flesh, her aubergine-coloured costume, the aubergine/black bar dividing the wall and the floor, and the unusual brown colour of the wall hanging, reiterated in the checkerboard – contrasts with the luminosity of the blue odalisque. Matisse varies the props – an Italian Rococo mirror, a plate of lemons and what appears to be a table on the left. He emphasises the model's pubic area with a dark triangle of shading that delineates the folds of her green harem pants. KB

Cat. 31 (RA ONLY)
Reclining Nude with Louis XIV Screen, 1923
Lithograph, 13 × 19 cm, on Chine paper, 28.7 × 37.6 cm
Victoria and Albert Museum, London

Cat. 32 (RA ONLY)
Nude on a Divan with a Moucharabieh Background, 1922
Lithograph, 50 × 40.5 cm, on Chine paper, 59.7 × 44 cm
Victoria and Albert Museum, London

Cat. 33 (RA ONLY)
Arabesque, 1924
Lithograph, 47.7 × 31.6 cm, on Chine paper, 59.4 × 43.2 cm
Victoria and Albert Museum, London

Cat. 34 (RA ONLY)
Seated Odalisque with a Tulle Skirt, 1924
Lithograph, 36.7 × 27 cm, on Chine paper, 50.8 × 36.7 cm
Victoria and Albert Museum, London

Cat. 35 (RA ONLY)
Standing Odalisque with a Tray of Fruit, 1924
Lithograph, 37.3 × 27.5 cm, on Japan paper, 48 × 33 cm
Victoria and Albert Museum, London

Cat. 36 (RA ONLY)
Large Odalisque with Bayadère Costume, 1925
Lithograph, 54.2 × 44 cm, on Chine paper, 70.3 × 55.4 cm
Victoria and Albert Museum, London

Cat. 37 (RA ONLY)
Odalisque with Red Satin Culottes, 1925
Lithograph, 18.7 × 26.7 cm, on Chine paper, 27.5 × 35.5 cm
Victoria and Albert Museum, London

Cat. 38 (RA ONLY)
Odalisque with a Bowl of Fruit, 1925
Lithograph, 31.5 × 24.5 cm, on Chine paper, 47 × 32.5 cm
Victoria and Albert Museum, London

Cat. 39 (RA ONLY)
Torso with Ewer, 1927
Lithograph, 37.7 × 26.5 cm, on Chine paper, 49.8 × 34.6 cm
Victoria and Albert Museum, London

Cat. 40 (RA ONLY)
Odalisque, Samovar and Bowl of Fruit, 1929
Lithograph, 28 × 37.5 cm, on vélin d'Arches, 38.2 × 57 cm
Victoria and Albert Museum, London

Cat. 41 (RA ONLY)
Reclining Nude with Bowl of Fruit, 1926
Lithograph, 43.6 × 54 cm, on Japan paper, 46.2 × 56 cm
Victoria and Albert Museum, London

In 1922 Matisse returned to lithography after a break of five years. Using black ink on stone, he created clear, compact images, strong in contrasts. He reproduced the themes of his paintings and sculpture – the nude, the odalisque and the dancer – furthering his research on the play between figure and background, albeit on a smaller scale. Matisse produced about ten to twenty lithographs a year, published in editions of 50 to satisfy the growing popular market for his sensual and decorative oriental subject-matter. Many of the lithographs were conceived as a series, for example *Ten Dancers*, published by Matisse's dealer Bernheim-Jeune in 1927.

The eleven images exhibited here display Matisse's characteristic lithographic techniques of the 1920s, one based on the arabesque (the ornamental) and the other on heavy outlining and shading (the sculptural). The arabesque derives from the textiles Matisse employed to transform his studio. The lithographs unite his meticulous drawing technique and oriental subject-matter, as in *Nude on a Divan with a Moucharabieh Background* (1922). A naturalistic nude with arms raised reclines on the striped chaise longue dividing the floral patterned wall from the oriental carpet. Matisse's return to lithography begins with the nude who seems to project outward from the patterned background.

In *Arabesque* (1924), his calligraphic line creates an all-over design that includes the model with the familiar features of Henriette Darricarrère, the embroidery of her sheer blouse, her breast, the floral material and the *moucharabieh* in the background as elements of a single unified design scheme. Sketchier still, the reclining nude model in *Reclining Nude with a Bowl of Fruit* (1926) is formed by a light arabesque line. The top of her head, like the floral motif on the wall, is cut off by the edge of the paper, as though she formed part of the textile design. Matisse also employs the arabesque in *Odalisque, Samovar and Bowl of Fruit* (1929), which contains all the elements of the studio stage-set. The scattered apples and the model's breasts have the same ornamental quality as the floral cushion, carpet, wall-hanging and *moucharabieh*. The vertical folds of the curtain on the left, matched by the fluting of the samovar and the stripes of the cushion, provide contrast.

In other lithographs Matisse uses heavy shading to produce a dramatic

chiaroscuro effect that emphasises the sculptural quality of the model and creates areas of luminous whiteness. The floral texiles lose their definition to become a series of tones that form a background emphasising the volumes of the figure, as in the small-format *Reclining Nude with Louis XIV Screen* (1923) and the classically inspired *Torso with Ewer* (1927).

When the heavily outlined figure is placed against a patterned background, the compact and almost abstract composition takes on a geometric quality, as in *Odalisque with Red Satin Culottes* (1925) and *Odalisque with a Bowl of Fruit* (1925). The same is true of *Seated Odalisque with a Tulle Skirt* (1924), based on the curve, and *Standing Odalisque with a Tray of Fruit* (1924), based on the rectangle. An important resolution of the figure/background problem is the large-format *Large Odalisque with Bayadère Costume* (1925). The odalisque is seated in an upholstered armchair, seen close up against an abstract black background. The black stripes of her harem pants and her hair are luminous against the grey, smudged tones of the drapery and her nude torso. 'Black is a force: I use black to simplify the construction,' Matisse said.[1] KB

1 Henri Matisse, 'Black is a Colour', 1946, trans. in Flam 1995, p. 165.

Cat. 42 (RA/NY)
Reclining Nude, 1935
Pen and black ink on white paper,
37.7 × 55 cm
Mr and Mrs Thomas Gibson

In 1935 Matisse created an important series of pen-and-ink drawings of nudes in his studio depicting the model Lydia Delectorskaya, his studio assistant. His move towards surface painting and the simplicity of precisely drawn signs is played out on the body of the nude and the patterned textiles used to drape his studio stage-set. In *Reclining Nude* the model poses face down in a contorted position, her body cut off at thigh level on the right-hand side. Lying on her side, she turns her face and pubic area towards

the viewer. Matisse portrays the relatively naturalistic nude with a few schematic lines that leave the white paper bare to indicate her pale body. Her reclining body occupies the top half of the drawing, while underneath her, a uniform leaf motif enclosed in parallel tracks of curving lines, lozenge and zigzag patterns define the fabric draped over her divan. In the work Matisse begins to develop the flat, simplified designs that can be translated to a larger surface. KB

Cat. 43 (NY ONLY)
Purple Robe and Anemones, 1937
Oil on canvas, 73.1 × 60.5 cm
The Baltimore Museum of Art, Baltimore,
The Cone Collection, formed by Dr Claribel
Cone and Miss Etta Cone of Baltimore,
Maryland (BMA 1950.261)

Odalisque with Yellow Persian Robe and Anemones and *Purple Robe and Anemones* are works of Matisse's Fauvist revival, a return to his pictorial achievements in colour and form, in the light of his experiments of the previous twenty years.[1] *Odalisque with Yellow Persian Robe* depicts a modern odalisque, the model Hélène Galitzine, who wears a purple striped Persian robe loosely draped over a short green printed skirt and a white blouse. The bright-coloured setting includes a Moorish table with an oversized vase containing red, purple-and-white anemones and textiles, the curtains represented by red-and-black vertical stripes and the covering of the divan by lavender and purple stripes. Heavy black outlining delineates the scalloped edge of the robe, the model's hair, the furnishings and flowers. A lavender polka dot and pink fabric – a cushion? – and a black-and-white grid – probably a schematic design of the wall tiles in the fourth floor studio at place Charles-Félix – appear in the centre of the painting.

The animated patterning, painted with broad brush strokes, provides a strong rhythm like 'musical harmony', as Matisse describes it, which, with the clashing colours, gives a direct, brash effect. The areas of ochre and purple in

the background flatten the work, creating an equal balance between figure and background.

Purple Robe and Anemones portrays a fair-haired model with a similar, though somewhat more restrained treatment, in an almost identical setting. The only difference appears to be the contrast of purple and green colours for the robe and table, and, in the background, red stripes on yellow on the left and pale blue with white arabesques on the right for the wall. A thinner, more controlled line for the patterning and the black tiled floor is also apparent. The strident colours of the striped background are picked up in the model's red floral-patterned divan and cushion. Although the construction of the two paintings of a model lounging in a striped Persian robe is similar, Matisse's varied orchestration of the woman, colours and patterning results in a strikingly different feeling. KB

1 See Henri Matisse, 'Statements to Tériade: The Purity of Means', 1936, trans. in Flam 1995, p. 122.

Cat. 44 (NY ONLY)
Small Odalisque in a Purple Robe, 1937
Oil on canvas, 38.1 × 45.7 cm
Private collection

Small Odalisque in a Purple Robe and *Red Robe and Violet Tulips*, completed in January and March 1937 respectively, form part of a series of decorative paintings of models wearing a Persian robe, surrounded by plants and flowers. During this phase of Matisse's work, colour and drawing vie for dominance in the construction of a painting. In *Small Odalisque*, the more muted of the two, the dark-haired model, her head surrounded by a crown of small yellow flowers, lounges with her right leg drawn up, on a pale, lavender-grey striped divan. The central focus of the work is her purple-striped Persian robe, which drapes and falls in curved or vertical stripes, thickly painted. Green harem pants and a pale-green blouse complete her ensemble. The green wall, striped divan and terracotta tiled floor reinforce the curves and verticals of the robe in fine etched lines. The solid yellow panel on the extreme left, which opens up another dimension of the work, contrasts strongly with the purples and greens.

In Red Robe and Violet Tulips the attempt to balance vibrant, Fauvist colour and drawing becomes more intense. The lavender harem pants, tulips, left background wall and plinth contrast with the reds of the robe and floor and the ochre of the wall and armchair. Large, green rhododendron leaves frame the dark-haired model's head. The design on her red robe is a calligraphic white script and the motif of the cushion a wild red print. Strong vertical lines form the background, black on the left and purple on the right, while the thinner diagonal lines of the red floor are etched in white. In both paintings, constructed through line and blocks of colour to give a flat, decorative effect, Matisse tries to resolve the dichotomy of drawing and colour in easel painting, an important stage on his way to creating mural art. KB

Cat. 45
Odalisque with Yellow Persian Robe and Anemones, 1937
Oil on canvas, 73 × 60 cm
Philadelphia Museum of Art, Philadelphia, The Samuel S. White 3rd and Vera White Collection, 1967

See cat. 43

Cat. 46 (NY ONLY)
Red Robe and Violet Tulips, 1937
Oil on canvas, 55 × 46 cm
Private collection

See cat. 44

Cat. 47 (NY ONLY)
Woman in Blue, 1937
Oil on canvas, 91 × 73 cm
Philadelphia Museum of Art, Philadelphia, gift of Mrs John Wintersteen

Woman in Blue sums up the new direction Matisse's art took in the mid-

1930s. 'Pictures which have become refinements, subtle gradations, dissolutions without energy, call for beautiful blues, reds, yellows – matter to stir the sensual depths in men,' as Matisse put it.[1] The documented states of Woman in Blue, dating from 26 February to the end of April 1937, reveal the increasingly linear construction of the work and the filling in of broad areas of colour, specifically blue, red and yellow.

In this audacious painting, the model Lydia Delectorskaya wears a blue puff-sleeved ball gown with white organdie ruffles made by her especially for Matisse to paint. Her courtly pose recalls that of the classical Portrait of Madame Moitessier by Ingres (1856; National Gallery, London). It is interesting to compare the painting with the photograph Matisse took of the same subject in his fourth floor studio at place Charles-Félix. He simplifies the curved shape of the dress and bench and the geometric patterning of the wall and floor, using a fine etched line to achieve a more abstract construction. The studio's false tile decoration, seen in the photograph, becomes a bright-red grid that meets the black lattice design of the floor. Three schematic drawings, cut off by the edges of the canvas, hang on the tiled wall. Matisse's clarity of line and use of broad areas of colour indicate his transition towards a painting of pure decoration on a monumental scale. KB

1 Flam 1995, p. 122.

Cat. 48 (RA ONLY)
Seated Girl in Persian Robe, 1942
Oil on canvas, 43 × 56 cm
Musée Picasso, Paris

Painted in December 1942, Seated Girl in Persian Robe was a gift from Matisse to Pablo Picasso, who, six months previously, had given the artist a portrait of his companion Dora Maar. During the war, Matisse, mainly confined to bed recovering from surgery, continued his research into the synthesis of drawing, colour and emotion. The painting portrays a fair-haired young girl, Monique Bourgeois, in a purple-striped

Persian robe and black-and-white striped skirt. She sits in Matisse's familiar antique armchair against a green patterned background of stylised petals or leaves traced in black crayon. In the work Matisse tries to balance drawing and colour. The linear construction of the painting indicates the dominance of drawing, while the colours remain separated and muted. In the flat, decorative painting, composed of verticals and curves, Matisse employs abstract patterning and signs for objects, such as the model's claw-shaped hands and broad areas of contrasting colour that can be translated to a larger surface. KB

Cat. 49
Hélène au Cabochon, 1937
Oil on canvas, 55 × 33 cm
Private collection

See cats 43 and 45

Cat. 50 (RA/NY)
The Green Romanian Blouse, 1939
Oil on canvas, 61 × 46 cm
Private collection

In The Green Romanian Blouse Matisse continues Matisse's series of the model in repose, dressed in an embroidered blouse and posed against an abstract background. The model in this painting is viewed close up, her figure cropped on either side like a photograph, making the background more abstract.

Matisse 'modulates' space with a thick, black line that forms arabesques, strong verticals and weaker horizontal stripes, as well as the familiar lozenge pattern, painted here in ochre and light green, for the floor. The line becomes a number '3' to define the model's upper lip and to trace a loose shape around the floral embroidery of her blouse. The heavy vertical bar indicating the tabletop cuts through the middle of the painting on the left, while the broad red curve of the sofa back leaps out of it. Thick, black vertical bars contain the washed blue colour in the background and thinner, curved black verticals delineate the blue upholstered back of the sofa. The black

line curves and dips to create the outline of the drop-neck blouse and its floral patterning against the green fabric. The year 1939 fell within a period of transition – from around 1937 to 1945 – for the artist to purely decorative mural compositions. On the way to creating large-scale decorative works, Matisse experiments with drawing and colour, two inimical forces, in easel painting. The Romanian blouse provides an area of confrontation between the forces of line and colour. KB

Cat. 51 (NY ONLY)
The Dream, 1940
Oil on canvas, 81 × 65 cm
Private collection

Matisse worked on The Dream for a whole year, completing the painting in September 1940 at the beginning of the Occupation of Nice. He refers to the length of time it took to finish it, indicating the importance of the process as much as the result. In the mid-1930s Matisse began to work in series or took a single painting through stages, allowing his original conception of the piece to unfold over time. In The Dream, which combines the themes of the sleeping woman and the Romanian blouse, he draws on the nude model's pose and the synthetic elements of his 1935 version, also entitled The Dream (in the Musée National d'Art Moderne, Centre Georges Pompidou, Paris), employing a calligraphic drawing style and vibrant Fauvist colours. Matisse transforms his original, more romantic conception of the sleeping woman wearing a Romanian blouse – Still-life with a Sleeping Woman (1940) in the National Gallery of Art, Washington DC – into the more stylised version of The Dream. For Matisse, the Romanian blouse is equivalent to a work of art: 'I found a beautiful Romanian blouse, of ancient design, with old ochre stitches, that must have belonged to a princess and I'd like many more of them, for which I'd willingly exchange a fine drawing.'[1] KB

1 Fourcade 1972, p. 185. Letter from Henri Matisse to Theodor Pallady, 1940–41.

Fig. 48
Henri Cartier-Bresson, Henri
Matisse in his studio, 1943–44.
Photograph

Chronology

HILARY SPURLING

Fig. 49
Henri Matisse, **Matisse at the Engraver's Stone**, 1900–03.
Drypoint, 32.9 × 51 cm. Musée Matisse, Nice-Cimiez

Fig. 50
Weaver at his loom, c. 1940s.
Photograph

1869   31 December: Matisse born at Le Cateau-Cambrésis, the grandson and great-grandson of weavers in a textile region famous from medieval times for its fine linen weaving.

1870   January: moves with his parents to Bohain-en-Vermandois, a textile town specialising ever since the invention of the Jacquard loom at the turn of the century in richly patterned cashmere shawls.

1870–71   War with Prussia ends in France's defeat at the battle of St-Quentin in January 1871.

1870–80   Economic recovery after the war leads to an explosion in the luxury textile trade. Bohain's silk weavers switch to producing material for the top end of the fashion market with 10,000 looms in the town and its immediate vicinity, working direct for Parisian fashion houses and department stores by the end of the decade. Matisse attends school successively in Bohain and Le Cateau.

1882–87   Moves to the lycée at St-Quentin, and comes into constant conflict with the school art department. Periodic illness prevents his sitting examinations, or working in his parents' seedstore.

1885   Builds a toy theatre and stages the *Eruption of Vesuvius* with himself as director, designer, scene painter and lighting specialist.

1887–89   Leaves school to study law in Paris; returns to St-Quentin to work as a lawyer's clerk.

1890–91   Rejection by the army for military service precipitates a final physical collapse. Recovers when presented by his mother with a paint box. Produces his first oil-painting, *Still-life with Books*, and goes to work for another lawyer in St-Quentin. Enrols for drawing lessons at the Ecole Quentin de La Tour, embroiled at the time in a running battle between the repressive academic discipline of the Ecole des Beaux-Arts and the innovative, experimental approach of local textile manufacturers. Becomes the star pupil of a breakaway painting academy founded by Emmanuel Croizé, and is expelled for subversion from the Ecole Quentin de La Tour. Leads a small group of rebels to Paris.

1891–95   Enrols briefly at the Académie Julian, and realises he will never be able to paint like other people. Taken on unofficially as a pupil by Gustave Moreau at the Ecole des Beaux-Arts; fails the entrance exam four times before eventually passing in 1895. Encouraged by Moreau to embark on an intensive programme of self-education in the Louvre. Finds lodgings at 19 quai St-Michel, and begins to assemble a textile collection from junk stalls around Notre-Dame.

1894   Birth of daughter Marguerite with Caroline Joblaud.

1895–97   Discovers Impressionism through Camille Pissarro in Paris and the Australian John Russell on the island of Belle-Ile. Influenced by Monet and Van Gogh. His work repudiated by Moreau. Caroline Joblaud leaves him. Meets Amélie Parayre.

Fig. 51
Emile Flamant, Fresco showing Bohain weavers and their luxury fabrics, 1925.
Fresco. L'Hôtel de Ville, Bohain

Fig. 52
Printed cotton fabric of the type supplied by I. V. Shchukin & Sons, c. 1890s

1898 January: marries Amélie Parayre. Leaves Paris with her for London, Corsica and Toulouse. Discovery of the South precipitates a first explosion of colour on his canvases.

1899 Birth of son Jean. Buys *Three Bathers* by Cézanne. Meets André Derain.

1900 *Woman Reading* turned down by the painting section of the Exposition Universelle; Bohain wins gold and silver medals, and the Grand Prix in the textile section. Birth of son Pierre.

1901 Shows seven paintings at the Salon des Indépendants.

1902 February: takes part in mixed show at Berthe Weill's gallery. May: eruption of the Humbert Scandal, a financial scam involving leading Third Republic politicians. Amélie Matisse's parents, the Humberts' confidential secretary and housekeeper, treated as scapegoats in the national press; Matisse's studio raided by police. Attempts unsuccessfully to earn a living for his destitute extended family from flower- and figure-painting. Organises the defence of his father-in-law, who is imprisoned in the Conciergerie.

1903 Takes refuge with his family in Bohain, living on his parents' charity; considers a job as colourist in a textile workshop. Returns to Paris for the Humbert trial. Exhibits two paintings at first Salon d'Automne. Buys the *toile de Jouy*.

1904 June: first one-man show at Ambroise Vollard's gallery. Spends summer in St-Tropez with Paul Signac and Henri Cross. Experiments with Divisionism.

1905 Shows *Luxe, Calme et Volupté* at Salon des Indépendants. Spends the first of many summers at Collioure with his family and Derain. Produces first Fauvist works, and exhibits them at the Salon d'Automne. Sells *Woman in a Hat* to Leo Stein. Sets up a studio in the Couvent des Oiseaux, Paris.

1906 March: one-man show at Druet gallery. Shows *Bonheur de vivre* at Salon des Indépendants. First meets Picasso, and introduces him to African art. May: spends two weeks in Algeria, bringing back several red, yellow and black prayer-mats from Biskra. Paints *Still-life with a Red Rug* and *Dishes and Fruit on red-and-black Rug* (cat. 8). Sergei Shchukin, head of a Russian textile empire, starts collecting Matisse's work, following in the footsteps of Sarah Stein, who, with her husband Michael, builds up an unrivalled collection of around fifty Matisses in the next two years.

1907 Shows *Blue Nude: Memory of Biskra* at the Salon des Indépendants. Visits Italy, and is powerfully affected by Giotto's frescoes at Padua. Paints *Le Luxe* (I) and *Le Luxe* (II) on his return. Begins to teach a small painting class (afterwards known as the Académie Matisse) in Paris that winter. December: moves family and studio to the Couvent du Sacré Coeur.

Fig. 53
Henri Matisse, **Bronze and Fruit**, 1907–08. Oil on canvas, 90 × 115 cm.
The Pushkin State Museum of Fine Arts, Moscow

Fig. 54
Henri Matisse, **Basket of Oranges**, 1912. Oil on canvas,
94 × 83 cm. Musée Picasso, Paris

1908　Paints *Bathers with a Turtle*, *Portrait of Greta Moll* (cat. 10) and *Harmony in Red* (fig. 2). Buys an oriental carpet and paints *Still-life in Venetian Red* and *Bronze and Fruit* (fig. 53). Shows for the first time in New York and Moscow. Publishes 'Notes of a Painter'.

1909　Paints *Still-life with Blue Tablecloth* (cat. 9). Commissioned by Shchukin to produce *Dance* and *Music*. Moves to Issy-les-Moulineaux that autumn, and signs a first contract with Galérie Bernheim-Jeune (who will remain his dealers until 1925).

1910　Begins the year with a retrospective at Bernheim-Jeune, and ends it by exhibiting in Roger Fry's first Post-Impressionist show in London. Shows *Dance* and *Music* at Salon d'Automne. Is chiefly impressed, at a major exhibition of Islamic art in Munich, by the hall containing 230 oriental carpets. Leaves for Spain to see the Alhambra at Granada. Receives five major commissions from Shchukin, and constructs *Seville Still-life* (cat. 11) and *Spanish Still-life* (fig. 36) around newly acquired Spanish textiles.

1911　Produces *The Pink Studio* and *The Painter's Family*, constructed respectively round a Spanish textile and an oriental carpet, both painted at Issy to commissions by Shchukin. Paints *The Red Studio* and *Interior with Aubergines*. Travels to Moscow in November to stay with Shchukin in Moscow, and accepts a further substantial series of commissions.

1912　Spends six weeks this spring painting in Tangier, starting with *Basket of Oranges* (fig. 54). Returns in the autumn for another four and a half months. The bulk of the Tangier paintings go to Moscow, and so do four large canvases painted at Issy that summer, including *Conversation* and *Goldfish*.

1913　Works on sculpture – *Back II* and *Jeanette v* – and the *Portrait of Madame Matisse* at Issy. Takes part in the travelling Armory show in New York, Boston and Chicago.

1914　Moves back to 19 quai St-Michel in January. Works with the English Bergsonian and aesthetic theorist, M.S. Prichard. Paints *Interior with a Goldfish Bowl* and *Portrait of Mlle Yvonne Landsberg*. House at Issy requisitioned as German armies threaten Paris on outbreak of war in August. Paints *French Window at Collioure*. Returns to Paris and is rejected by the army.

1915–16　Organises aid for starving compatriots behind German lines in Bohain. House at Issy becomes a shelter for soldiers and non-combatants, including Juan Gris and Gino Severini. Paints a series of sombre, semi-abstract works culminating in *Piano Lesson* and *Bathers by a River*.

1917　Works with an Italian model Lorette. Visits his son Jean in army training camp near Marseilles in December, moving on to Nice for a stay of few days that lengthens to six months.

1918　January: two-man show with Picasso at Galérie Paul Guillaume in Paris.

Fig. 55
Matisse in his studio at place Charles-Félix,
Nice, with two North African hangings in the
background. Photograph. Matisse Archives, Paris

Fig. 56
Lydia Delectorskaya modelling the dress from Woman in Blue, 1937.
Photograph. Philadelphia Museum of Art, Philadelphia

Establishes a pattern for the next twenty years, spending summers with his family at Issy, and winter painting seasons in Nice. Begins to build up a portable painting wardrobe, buying couture clothes for his wife and daughter from Germaine Bongard.

1919 Works with the model Antoinette Arnoud. One-man show at Galérie Bernheim-Jeune (where he will continue to show until 1924). Persuaded by Sergei Diaghilev to travel to London in the autumn to design the ballet Le Chant du rossignol, using a scale-model theatre, and cutting décor and costumes out of painted paper (cat. 82).

1920 Rossignol première in Paris and London. Summer with his wife and daughter at Etretat.

1921–27 Antoinette succeeded as principal model by Henriette Darricarrère, who initiates a long series of odalisque paintings in oriental outfits based initially on Bakst's costumes for the ballet Shéhérezade.

Matisse expands his costume wardrobe with a repertoire of Moroccan robes, blouses and jackets. Moves into two rented rooms in an apartment block at 1 place Charles-Félix, Nice (where he will remain, acquiring steadily more space, until 1938). Transforms successive studios into workspace as flexible as a film or stage-set with the help of his 'working library', a constantly expanding collection of fabric screens, hangings, curtains, spreads and cushions. Ongoing experiments with light and colour culminate in Decorative Figure on an Ornamental Ground (cat. 26). Principal collectors are the Americans Dr Albert Barnes from Philadelphia and two textile-loving sisters, Claribel and Etta Cone of Baltimore.

1927 Retrospective organised by his son Pierre Matisse at Valentine Dudensing Gallery in New York. Paints Henriette for the last time. Shifts his home base to Nice, but retains a flat at 132 Boulevard Montparnasse, Paris. Wins first prize at the Carnegie International Exhibition, Pittsburgh.

1928–29 Period of transition marked by fewer oil-paintings and increased printmaking. Wife's health declines.

1930 Visits the USA three times. Spends ten weeks in Tahiti, returning home with a collection of Polynesian barkcloth or tapas and printed cotton pareos. Agrees to paint a mural for the Barnes Foundation at Merion near Philadelphia.

1931 Major retrospectives at Galérie Petit, Paris, and the new Museum of Modern Art in New York.

1931–34 Invents technique of cut-paper patterns for work on the Barnes commission. Employs Lydia Delectorskaya as studio assistant. Installs the Dance at Merion in 1933, and produces an alternative version (later bought by the city of Paris).

1935–37 Returns to oil-painting. Delectorskaya models for the Pink Nude, Woman in Blue and other works. Makes a tapestry cartoon based on the painting Window at Tahiti.

Fig. 57
Henri Matisse, **The Romanian Blouse**, 1939–40.
Oil on canvas, 92 × 73 cm. Musée National d'Art Moderne,
Centre Georges Pompidou

Fig. 58
Henri Matisse, **Interior with an Egyptian Curtain**,
1948. Oil on canvas, 116.2 × 89.2 cm. Phillips Collection,
Washington DC

1938   Exhibition at the Paul Rosenberg gallery in Paris. Buys six couture dresses in a Paris sale. Moves into an apartment block in the former Hotel Régina at Cimiez above Nice. Munich crisis: sends his wife to safety in Toulouse, and remains behind to evacuate Nice apartment.

1939   Amélie Matisse leaves her husband. Première of Le Rouge et le noir (L'Etrange Farandole), designed as a virtually abstract ballet for Léonide Massine. Matisse joined by Lydia Delectorskaya in Paris that autumn as France declares war on Germany. Paints a series of Romanian blouses (cat. 50 and fig. 57).

1940   May: flees with the rest of the population from Hitler's armies advancing on Paris. After French surrender, gradually heads back to Nice by autumn, travelling across France. Already seriously ill.

1941–42 Emergency colostomy at Lyons in January 1941. Remains at risk for twelve months, and thereafter a permanent invalid. Works in bed on drawings, illustrated books and an inventive series of seated female models.

1943   Forced to evacuate Nice. Moves to a rented villa in Vence. Hangs his walls with Kuba cloths from Zaire, and makes his first paper cut-outs for the album Jazz.

1944   April: wife and daughter arrested by Gestapo; Amélie imprisoned, Marguerite discovered only after the Liberation of France in August to have survived interrogation and torture.

1945   Retrospective at Salon d'Automne, Paris. Issue of Verve devoted to Matisse. Inaugural one-man show at Galérie Maeght in Paris and joint showing with Picasso at Victoria and Albert Museum, London. French State buys six paintings.

1946–47 Paints final series of Vence interiors, covers his walls with compositions in cut-paper, and designs two wall-sized screen prints, Oceania: The Sky, and Oceania: The Sea. Makes two parallel tapestry designs, Polynesia: The Sky and Polynesia: The Sea, for the Gobelins workshops. Publication of Jazz.

1948–51 Works on the only decorative commission ever offered him in France, the Chapel of the Rosary for Dominican nuns at Vence, designing stained-glass windows from full-size cut-paper maquettes.

1948   Retrospective at Philadelphia Museum of Art. Paints a final semi-abstract series of interiors, including Interior with Egyptian Curtain (fig. 58).

1949   Moves back to Cimiez. Exhibition to mark his eightieth birthday at the new Musée National d'Art Moderne in Paris.

1950   Works on large-scale paper cut-outs. Wins first prize at 25th Venice Biennale. Exhibits chapel designs at Maison de la Pensée Française in Paris.

1951   Retrospectives at Museum of Modern Art, New York, and National Museum of Tokyo.

1952–54 Makes Blue Nude cut-outs, La Tristesse du roi, The Parakeet and the Mermaid, and designs various stained-glass windows in cut paper.

1953   Musée Matisse opens in Le Cateau-Cambrésis.

1954   Dies in Nice on 3 November, and is buried at Cimiez.

Fig. 59
Brassaï, Interior of Matisse's
Villa Le Rêve, Vence, with his
'toile de Jouy' beside the fireplace,
1946. Photograph

Fig. 60
Henri Cartier-Bresson, Matisse at his Villa Le Rêve, Vence, with Kuba cloths and a Tahitian *tapa* or barkcloth in the background, 1943–44. Photograph

Select Bibliography

ARAGON 1972
Louis Aragon, Henri Matisse: A Novel, trans. by Jack Stewart, London, 1972

BARR 1975
Alfred Barr, Matisse: His Art and His Public, London, 1975

CHICAGO 1994
Odilon Redon 1840–1916, Douglas W. Druick (ed.), The Art Institute of Chicago; Van Gogh Museum, Amsterdam; Royal Academy of Arts, London, 1994

CLEVENOT 1994
Dominique Clévenot, Une Esthétique du voile. Essai sur l'art arabo-islamique, Paris, 1994

COPENHAGEN 1999
Henri Matisse. Four Great Collectors, Albert Kostenevich et al. (eds), exh. cat., Statens Museum for Kunst, Copenhagen, 1999

COURTHION A
Pierre Courthion, 'Conversations avec Henri Matisse', unpublished TS, Getty Center for the History of Art, Santa Monica, California

COURTHION B
Pierre Courthion, miscellaneous papers, Getty Center for the History of Art, Santa Monica, California

COX 1900
Raymond Cox, L'Art de décorer les tissus, d'après les collections du Musée historique de la Chambre de commerce de Lyon, Paris and Lyons, 1900

DAFTARI 1991
Fereshteh Daftari, The Influence of Persian Art on Gauguin, Matisse and Kandinsky, New York and London, 1991

DELECTORSKAYA 1988
Lydia Delectorskaya, With Apparent Ease: Henri Matisse. Drawings and Paintings 1935–1939, trans. by Olga Tourkoff, Paris, vol. I, 1988 (original French edition, 1986)

DELECTORSKAYA 1996
Lydia Delectorskaya, Henri Matisse. Contre vents et marées. Peinture et livres illustrés de 1939 à 1943, Paris, 1996

DEMAISON 1907
Maurice Demaison, 'L'Exposition des tissus et des miniatures d'Orient au Musée des arts décoratifs', Les Arts, Paris, May 1907, pp. 29–43

DENIS 1905
Maurice Denis, 'La Peinture', L'Ermitage, Paris, 15 November 1905, in Le Ciel et l'Arcadie, Jean-Paul Bouillon (ed.), Paris, 1993, pp. 84–98

FLAM 1973
Jack Flam, Matisse on Art, London and New York, 1973

FLAM 1995
Jack Flam, Matisse on Art, Berkeley and Los Angeles, 1995

FLAM 2003
Jack Flam, Matisse and Picasso: The Story of Their Rivalry and Friendship, New York, 2003

FOURCADE 1972
Dominique Fourcade (ed.), Henri Matisse. Ecrits et propos sur l'art, Paris, 1972

FRANKFURT 2002
Henri Matisse: Drawing with Scissors. Masterpieces from the Late Years, Olivier Berggruen and Max Hollein (eds), exh. cat., Schirn Kunsthalle Frankfurt; Nationalgalerie, Sammlung Berggruen, Staatlichen Museen zu Berlin, 2002–03

FRY 1910
Roger Fry, 'The Munich Exhibition of Mohammedan Art', The Burlington Magazine, London, July–September 1910; in Vision and Design, J. B. Bullen (ed.), Mineola, 1981 (original edition, 1920), pp. 81–91

GIMARET 1988
Daniel Gimaret, Les Noms divins en Islam. Exégèse lexicographique et théologique, Paris, 1988

GRABAR 1973
Oleg Grabar, La Formation de l'art islamique, Paris, 1987 (original English edition, 1973)

JACQUES-MARIE 1993
Sister Jacques-Marie, Henri Matisse. La Chapelle de Vence, Nice, 1993

KAISERSLAUTERN 1989
Matisse und seine deutschen Schüler, Gisela Fiedler-Bender, exh. cat., Pfalzgalerie, Kaiserslautern, Germany, 1989

KELEKIAN 1909
Dikran Khan Kelekian, The Potteries of Persia. Being a Brief History of the Art of Ceramics in the Near East, Paris, 1909

KOSTENEVICH AND SEMENOVA 1993
Albert Kostenevich and Natalia Semenova, Collecting Matisse, Paris, 1993 (French edition, 1993)

KUHNEL 1910
Ernst Kühnel, 'Die Ausstellung Mohammedanischer Kunst München 1910', Münchner Jahrbuch der bildenden Kunst, Munich, 1910, pp. 211–51

KUHNEL 1949
Ernst Kühnel, Die Arabeske, Wiesbaden, 1949

LABRUSSE 1998
Rémi Labrusse, 'Paris, capitale des arts de l'Islam? Quelques aperçus sur la formation des collections françaises d'art islamique au tournant du siècle', Bulletin de la société de l'histoire de l'art français, Paris, 1998, pp. 275–311

LABRUSSE 1999
Rémi Labrusse, Matisse. La condition de l'image, Paris, 1999

LABRUSSE AND PODZEMSKAIA 2000
Rémi Labrusse and Nadia Podzemskaia, 'Naissance d'une vocation. Aux sources de la carrière byzantine de Thomas Whittemore', Dumbarton Oaks Papers, Washington DC, 2000, no. 54, pp. 43–69

LAVOIX 1878
Henri Lavoix, 'La Galerie Orientale du Trocadéro', La Gazette des Beaux-Arts, Paris, XVIII, 1878, pp. 769–91

LE CATEAU-CAMBRESIS 1998
Matisse et l'Océanie. Le voyage à Tahiti, Dominique Szymusiak (ed.), exh. cat., Musée Matisse, Le Cateau-Cambrésis, 1998

LENINGRAD 1969
Matisse, exh. cat., State Hermitage Museum, Leningrad, 1969

LEVY 1976
Pierre Lévy, Des Artistes et un collectionneur, Paris, 1976

LOEB 1945
Pierre Loeb, Voyages à travers la peinture, Paris, 1945

MASSIGNON 1921
Louis Massignon, 'Les Méthodes de réalisation artistique des peuples de l'Islam', Syria, Paris, April 1921; in Opera minora, Youakim Moubarak (ed.), Beirut, vol. III, 1963, pp. 9–24

MATISSE 1908
Henri Matisse, 'Notes d'un peintre', La Grande Revue, Paris, 25 December 1908; in Flam 1995, pp. 30–43

MATISSE 1939
Henri Matisse, 'Notes of a Painter on His Drawing', Le Point, July 1939; in Flam 1995, pp. 129–32

MATISSE 1947
Henri Matisse, 'Le Chemin de la couleur', topics gathered by Gaston Diehl, Art Présent, Paris, 1947; in Flam 1995, pp. 177–8

MATISSE, COUTURIER AND RAYSSIGUIER 1993
Henri Matisse, M.-A. Couturier and L.-B. Rayssiguier, La Chapelle de Vence. Journal d'une création, Paris, 1993

MIGEON 1903A
Gaston Migeon, Exposition des arts musulmans au musée des arts décoratifs, a selection of 100 photographic plates, Librairie Centrale des Beaux-Arts, Paris, 1903

MIGEON 1903B
Gaston Migeon, 'L'Exposition des arts musulmans', Les Arts, Paris, May 1903, pp. 1–34

MIGEON 1907
Gaston Migeon, Manuel d'art musulman. II. Arts plastiques et industriels, Paris, 1907

MIGEON 1909
Gaston Migeon, Les Arts du tissu, Paris, 1909

MONOD-FONTAINE, BALDASSARI AND LAUGIER 1989
Isabelle Monod-Fontaine, Anne Baldassari and Claude Laugier, Oeuvres de Henri Matisse, Paris, 1989

OSLO 1918
Modern French Painting, exh. cat., Kunstnerforbundet, Oslo, 1918

OSTHAUS 1971
Herta Hesse-Frielinghaus, August Hoff, et al., Karl Ernst Osthaus. Leben und Werk, Recklinghausen, 1971

PARIS 1989
Matisse, les collections du musée national d'art moderne, Isabelle Monod-Fontaine, exh. cat., Musée National d'Art Moderne, Centre Georges Pompidou, Paris, 1989

PARIS 1993
Henri Matisse 1904–1917, Dominique Fourcade and Isabelle Monod-Fontaine (eds), exh. cat., Musée National d'Art Moderne, Centre Georges Pompidou, Paris, 1993

PARIS 1998
Trésors fatimides du Caire, Brahim Alaoui, Farouk S. Asker, Marianne Barrucand and Karim Beddek (eds), exh. cat., Institut du Monde Arabe, Paris, 1998

PUY 1910
Michel Puy, Le Dernier Etat de la peinture. Les successeurs des Impressionnistes, Paris, 1910

REDON 1923
Lettres d'Odilon Redon 1878–1916, Paris and Brussels, 1923

RIEGL 1889
Alois Riegl, Die ägyptischen Textilfunde im K.K. österreichisches Museum für Kunst und Industrie. Allgemeine Charakteristik und Katalog, Vienna, 1889

RIEGL 1891
Alois Riegl, Altorientalische Teppiche, Leipzig, 1891

RIEGL 1893
Alois Riegl, Questions de style, Paris, 1992 (original edition, 1893)

RIEGL 1898
Alois Riegl, Grammaire historique des arts plastiques, Paris, 1978 (original manuscript, 1897–98)

RIEGL 1901
Alois Riegl, Spätrömische Kunstindustrie, Darmstadt, 1987 (original edition, 1901)

ROME 1997
Henri Matisse. 'La révélation m'est venue de l'Orient', Claude Duthuit, Albert Kostenevich, Rémi Labrusse and Jean Leymarie (eds), exh. cat., Musei Capitolini, Rome, 1997

ROXBURGH 2000
David J. Roxburgh, 'Au Bonheur des Amateurs: Collecting and Exhibiting Islamic Art, c. 1880–1910', Ars Orientalis. Exhibiting the Middle East. Collections and Perceptions of Islamic Art, Linda Komaroff (ed.), University of Michigan, 2000, vol. XXX, pp. 9–38

SARRE AND MARTIN 1910
Ausstellung von Meisterwerken muhammedanischer Kunst. Amtlicher Katalog, Friedrich Sarre and Fredrick Robert Martin (eds), Munich, 1910

SARRE AND MARTIN 1912
Die Ausstellung von Meisterwerken muhammedanischer Kunst in München 1910, Friedrich Sarre and Fredrick Robert Martin (eds), 3 vols, Munich, 1912

SCHERB 1910
Jean-François Scherb, 'Exposition Henri Matisse (Galerie Bernheim-Jeune)', Chronique des arts et de la curiosité, Paris, 19 February 1910, p. 59

SCHNEIDER 1984
Pierre Schneider, Matisse, trans. by Michael Taylor and Bridget Stevens Romer, London, 1984

SCHNEIDER 2001
Pierre Schneider, Petite Histoire de l'infini en peinture, Paris, 2001

SEMBAT 1920
Marcel Sembat, Henri Matisse, Paris, 1920

SEMENOVA 2004
Natalia Semenova, Collecting Genius. Sergei Shchukin and Early Modern Art, Washington DC, 2004

SHREVE SIMPSON 2000
Marianna Shreve Simpson, '"A Gallant Era": Henry Walters, Islamic Art and the Kelekian Connection', Ars Orientalis. Exhibiting the Middle East. Collections and Perceptions of Islamic Art, Linda Komaroff (ed.), University of Michigan, 2000, vol. XXX, pp. 91–112

SIGNAC 1899
Paul Signac, D'Eugène Delacroix au néo-impressionnisme, Françoise Cachin (ed.), Paris, 1987 (original edition, 1899)

SPURLING 1998
Hilary Spurling, The Unknown Matisse. A Life of Henri Matisse: The Early Years, 1869–1908, London and New York, 1998 (French edition, 2001)

SPURLING 2005
Hilary Spurling, Matisse the Master. A Life of Henri Matisse: The Conquest of Colour, 1909–1954, London and New York, 2005

TSCHUDI 1996
Manet bis Van Gogh. Hugo von Tschudi und der Kampf um die Moderne, Johann Georg Prinz von Hohenzollern and Peter-Klaus Schuster (eds), Munich and New York, 1996

VAUDOYER 1907
Jean-Louis Vaudoyer, 'Les Tissus musulmans', Art et décoration, Paris, February 1907, pp. 51–60

VERDET 1952
André Verdet, Prestiges de Matisse, Paris, 1952

WASHINGTON DC 1986
The Early Years in Nice 1916–30, Dominique Fourcade and Jack Cowart (eds), exh. cat., National Gallery of Art, Washington DC, 1986

Lenders to the Exhibition · Photographic Acknowledgements

LENDERS TO THE EXHIBITION

We are extremely grateful to the following lenders and to those private collectors who wish to remain anonymous:

Baltimore Museum of Art
Berne: Kunstmuseum
Bucharest: Muzeul National de Artă
al României
Cambridge, Mass.: Harvard University,
Fogg Art Museum
Copenhagen: Statens Museum for Kunst
Geneva: Musée d'Art et d'Histoire
Mr and Mrs Thomas Gibson
The Alex Hillman Family Foundation
Houston: The Menil Collection
Le Cateau-Cambrésis: Musée
départemental Matisse
London: The National Gallery
London: Thomas Gibson Fine Art Ltd
London: Victoria and Albert Museum
Lyons: Musée des Beaux-Arts
Moscow: The Pushkin State Museum
of Fine Arts
New Haven: Yale University Art Gallery
New York: The Metropolitan Museum
of Art
New York: Pierre and Maria Gaetana
Matisse Foundation Collection
Paris: Musée National d'Art Moderne,
Centre Georges Pompidou
Paris: Musée National de l'Orangerie
Paris: Musée Picasso
Philadelphia Museum of Art
Musée de Pontoise
Collection Carol Selle
St Petersburg: The State Hermitage
Museum
Stockholm: Moderna Museet
Wellesley, Mass.: Davis Museum and
Cultural Center, Wellesley College

PHOTOGRAPHIC ACKNOWLEDGEMENTS

COPYRIGHT OF WORKS ILLUSTRATED
The artists, their heirs and assigns, 2004
All illustrated works by Henri Matisse:
© Succession H. Matisse/DACS
2004
© Estate Brassaï – RMN: fig. 59
© Man Ray Trust/AGAGP, Paris,
2004: p. 2
© Succession Picasso/DACS, 2004:
fig: 15

PHOTOGRAPHIC CREDITS
All works of art are reproduced by
kind permission of their owners.
Specific acknowledgements are
as follows:

© AKG Images: fig. 17
© Artothek: figs 26, 34
Baltimore, The Baltimore Museum
of Art: cats 19, 24, 30, 43, 57
Basel, Kunstmuseum Basel: fig. 20
Basel, Photo Kunstmuseum Basel,
Martin Bühler: fig. 27
Photo Maurice Bérard: figs 43, 44
Philip Bernard: cat. 62
Courtesy Georges Bourgeois: figs 3, 5
and 50
© Estate Brassaï – RMN: fig. 59
© Bridgeman Art Library: figs 7, 14, 18,
19, 58
Steve Briggs: cat. 72
Bucharest, Muzeul National de Artă
al României: cats 58, 60
© Henri Cartier-Bresson/Magnum
Photos: figs 1, 48, 60
Christopher Burke: cats 70, 71, 78
Cambridge, Mass., © 2004 The
President and Fellows of Harvard
University: cat. 55

© Robert Capa R/Magnum Photos:
fig. 35
Photo François Fernandez: fig. 6
Florence, © 1990, Scala: cat. 12
Claude Gaspari: cats 3, 63
Geneva, © Musée d'Art et
d'Histoire/Maurice Aeschimann: cat. 82
Giraudon/Bridgeman Art Library: cat. 15
Patrick Goetelen: cat. 6
John Hammond: p. 4 (top left, top right,
bottom left), p. 5 (bottom right), p. 8,
pp. 10–11, p. 12, p. 70, p. 71, p. 72 (top
right, top left, bottom right), p. 80,
p. 83 (top), p. 99, p. 100, p. 101, p. 102,
p. 104, p. 105 (top, centre, bottom),
p. 106, p. 107, p. 154, p. 157, p. 158 (left),
p. 176 (top left, top right, bottom left,
bottom right), p. 177 (right, bottom
left), p. 178, p. 194 (top), p. 195 (top),
p. 198
Houston, Hickey-Robertson: cat. 81
Peter Lauri: cat. 21
Le Cateau-Cambrésis, © Museé
Matisse/D.R.: p. 161; Musée départ-
mental Matisse, Le Cateau-Cambrésis:
fig. 51
Levallois: cat. 1. London, courtesy
Thomas Gibson Fine Art: cats 42, 73
London, © V&A Picture Library: cats 31,
32, 33, 34, 35, 36, 37, 38, 39, 40, 41
Robert Lorenzson: cat. 20
Lyons, © Studio Basset: cats 64, 65, 66,
67, 68, 69
Todd May Photography: p. 4 (bottom
right), p. 5 (top left, top right, bottom
left), p. 72 (bottom left), p. 83 (bottom),
p. 96, p. 103, p. 158 (right), p. 159,
p. 160, p. 177 (top left), p. 194 (bottom),
p. 195 (bottom)
© Claude Mercier: cat. 50

New York, courtesy Acquavella Galleries:
cats 27, 44, 46
New York, courtesy J M K Gallery:
cats 53, 79
New York, courtesy Nancy Whyte Fine
Arts Inc.: cat. 74
New York, courtesy Sotheby's: cat. 76
New York, courtesy Yoshii Gallery:
cat. 75
Photograph © New York,
The Metropolitan Museum of Art:
cats 5, 22, 23, 28;
© 2004: cats 16, 77, 80
Nice, Photo Ville de Nice – Service
photographique: figs 40, 41, 42, 45, 49
Paris, © CNAC/MNAM Dist.
RMN/Adam Rzepka: cat. 26; ©
RMN/© René-Gabriel Ojéda: cat. 48
Hans Petersen: cat. 18
Philadelphia, Philadelphia Museum
of Art/Graydon Wood: cats 45, 47
© Philadelphia, Museum of Art:
fig. 28
© Beth Phillips: cat. 46
© Photo RMN/Jaqueline Hyde: fig. 4
© Photo RMN/Jean-Claude Planchet:
fig. 57
© Photo RMN/J. G. Berizzi: figs 15, 54
© Photo RMN/Lagiewski, fig. 30
Private collection, New York: fig. 8
© Photo SCALA, Florence: figs 2, 9, 11,
13, 21, 23, 24, 25, 36, 53
St Petersburg, © The State Hermitage
Museum: cats 7, 8, 9, 11
© G. Schiavinotto: cat. 51
Stockholm, SKM: cat. 29
Washington, Image © Board of
Trustees, National Gallery of Art
Washington, 1924: fig. 22

· 210 ·

Index

All references are to page numbers: those in **bold** type indicate illustrations

Benefactors of the Royal Academy of Arts

A Fulton Company Limited
Jacqueline and Jonathan Gestetner
The David Gill Memorial Fund
Patricia Glasswell
Michael Godbee
Mrs Alexia Goethe
Sir Nicholas and Lady Goodison
Piers and Rosie Gough
Ms Angela Graham
Sir Ronald Grierson
Sir Ewan and Lady Harper
Mr and Mrs Jocelin Harris
Mr Roger Hatchell and Mrs Ira Kettner
David and Lesley Haynes
Robin Heller Moss
Mrs Jonathan Hindle
Russell and Gundula Hoban
Anne Holmes-Drewry
Sir Joseph Hotung
Mrs Sue Howes and Mr Greg Dyke
Mr and Mrs Allan Hughes
Mrs Pauline Hyde
Simone Hyman
Mr S Isern-Feliu
Sir Martin and Lady Jacomb
Heather Angelien James
Mrs Ian Jay
Harold and Valerie Joels
Joseph Strong Frazer Trust
Mr D H Killick
Dr Rudolph King
Mr and Mrs James Kirkman
Mrs Ella Krasner
Joan H Lavender
Mr George Lengvari and Mrs Inez Lengvari
The Lady Lever of Manchester
Colette and Peter Levy
The Peter and Susan Lewis Foundation
Mrs Rose-Marie Lieberman
Mr and Mrs Kenneth Lieberman
Sir Sidney Lipworth QC and Lady Lipworth
Miss R Lomax-Simpson
London's Museums, Archives and Libraries Fund
Mr and Mrs Mark Loveday
Mr and Mrs Henry Lumley
Miss Jane McAusland
Mr and Mrs McCann
Gillian McIntosh
Mr and Mrs Andrew McKinna
Sally and Donald Main
Mrs Marilyn Maklouf
Mr and Mrs Eskandar Maleki
Mr and Mrs Michael (RA) and Jose Manser
Mr Curt Marcus
Mr Marcus Margulies
Mr David Marks and Ms Nada Chelhot
The Lord Marks of Broughton
Marsh Christian Trust
Mr and Mrs Stephen Mather
Lakshman Menon and Darren Rickards
The Mercers' Company
Mrs Kathryn Michael
Mr Roy Miles
The Millichope Foundation
Mrs Alan Morgan
Mr and Mrs Carl Anton Muller
Elaine and David Nordby
N Peal Cashmere
Mrs Elin Odfjell
Mr and Mrs Simon Oliver
Mrs Lale Orge
Mr Michael Palin
Mr and Mrs Vincenzo Palladino
Gerald Parkes
John H Pattison
The Pennycress Trust
Mr and Mrs Andrew S Perloff
Philip S Perry

John and Scheherazade Pesaute-Mullis
Mr David Pike
Mr Godfrey Pilkington
Mr and Mrs Anthony Pitt-Rivers
Mr and Mrs William A Plapinger
John Porter Charitable Trust
Miss Victoria Provis and Dick van der Broek
The Quercus Trust
John and Anne Raisman
Sir David and Lady Ramsbotham
Mr and Mrs Graham Reddish
Mr T H Reitman
The Family Rich Charities Trust
The Roland Group of Companies Plc
Mr and Mrs Ian Rosenberg
Sarah and Alastair Ross-Goobey
Paul and Jill Ruddock
Mrs Jean Sainsbury
Lady (Robert) Sainsbury
Mr and Mrs Bryan Sanderson
Mr and Mrs Hugh Sassoon
Mr S Schaefer and Mrs O Ma
The Schneer Foundation Inc
Carol Sellars
Mr and Mrs Kevin Senior
Mr and Mrs Marcus Setchell
Dr and Mrs Augustin Sevilla
Dr Lewis Sevitt
The Countess of Shaftesbury
Jonathan and Gillie Shaw
Mrs Stella Shawzin
P Simon
Simon Gillespie Restoration Studio
Alan and Marianna Simpson
George Sivewright
Mr and Mrs Mark Franklin Slaughter
Brian D Smith
Mr and Mrs David T Smith
Mrs Elayne Stilling
The Peter Storrs Trust
Summers Art Gallery, Dorking
Mrs D Susman
The Swan Trust
J A Tackaberry
Mrs Mark Tapley
The Tavolozza Foundation
Mr and Mrs John D Taylor
Miss M L Ulfane
Visa Lloyds Bank Monte Carlo
Mrs Catherine Vlasto
Mrs Claire Vyner
Bruno Wang
John B Watton
Edna and Willard Weiss
Rachel and Anthony Williams
Mr Jeremy Willoughby OBE
Manuela and Iwan Wirth
The Rt Hon Lord and Lady Young of Graffham
and others who wish to remain anonymous

BENJAMIN WEST GROUP DONORS
Chairman
Lady Judge

Gold Donors
Mrs Deborah L Brice
Jack and Linda Keenan
Riggs Bank Europe

Silver Donors
Lady Campbell Adamson
Ms Ruth Anderson
Susan Ansley Johnson
Mrs Adrian Bowden
Mr Jeffrey Brummette and Mrs Donna Lancia
Mr and Mrs Paul Collins
Lady Judge
Sir Paul Judge
Mr Scott Lanphere
Sir William and Lady Purves

Mr and Mrs Nicolas Rohatyn
Mrs Anne Sixt
Ms Tara Stack
Frederick and Kathryn Uhde

Bronze Donors
Sir Rudolph and Lady Agnew
Michael and Barbara Anderson
Mrs Alan Artus
Mr Oren Beeri and Mrs Michal Berkner
Tom and Diane Berger
Mr and Mrs Mark Booth
Wendy M Brooks and Tim Medland
Donald R Caldwell
Mrs Susanne Childs
Paolo Cicchiné and Marcelle Joseph
Mr Ed Cohen
Mrs Joan Curci
Linda and Ronald F Daitz
Mr and Mrs C R Dammers
Mr and Mrs Peter Dicks
Virginia H Drabbe-Seeman
Eversheds
Arthur Fabricant
Mr Joseph A Field
Mr and Mrs Robert L Forbes
Cyril and Christine Freedman
Mr and Mrs Edward Greene
Madeleine Hodgkin
Suzanne and Michael Johnson
Mr and Mrs Richard Kaufman
Lorna Klimt
Mr Charles G Lubar
Mr and Mrs Michael Mackenzie
Mr and Mrs Bruce McLaren
Mike and Martha Pedersen
Ann Dell Prevost
Carole Turner Record
Mr and Mrs Philip Renaud
Mr and Mrs K M Rubie
Mr and Mrs Justus Roele
Mrs Sylvia B Scheuer
Mr and Mrs Thomas Schoch
Carl Stewart
John and Sheila Stoller
LA Tanner & Co, Inc
Mr and Mrs Julian Treger
Michael and Yvonne Uva
Mr and Mrs Jeffrey Weingarten
Mr and Mrs John D Winter
and others who wish to remain anonymous

SCHOOLS PATRONS GROUP
Chairman
Mrs Alison Myners

Gold Patrons
Arts and Humanities Research Board
The Brown Foundation, Inc., Houston
The Gilbert & Eileen Edgar Foundation
The Eranda Foundation
The Ernest Cook Trust
Mr and Mrs Jack Goldhill
Fiona Johnstone
The David Lean Foundation
The Leverhulme Trust
The Henry Moore Foundation
Newby Trust Limited
Edith and Ferdinand Porjes Charitable Trust
The Rose Foundation
Paul Smith and Pauline Denyer-Smith
The South Square Trust
The Starr Foundation
Sir Siegmund Warburg's Voluntary Settlement
The Harold Hyam Wingate Foundation

Silver Patrons
The Lord Aldington
The Stanley Picker Trust
The Radcliffe Trust
The Celia Walker Art Foundation

Bronze Patrons
The Charlotte Bonham-Carter Charitable Trust
Mr and Mrs Stephen Boyd
The Selina Chenevière Foundation
May Cristea Award
Keith and Pam Dawson
The Delfont Foundation
Mr Alexander Duma
Hirsh London
Mrs Juliette Hopkins
Ken and Dora Howard
The Lark Trust
The late Mrs Lore Lehmann
Mrs Peter Low
Martineau Family Charity
Claus and Susan Moehlmann
Mrs Alison Myners
Mr and Mrs Carlo Nicolai
N Peal Cashmere
Pickett
Peter Rice Esq
Mr and Mrs Anthony Salz
Mr and Mrs Robert Lee Sterling Jr
The Peter Storrs Trust
Mr and Mrs Denis Tinsley
Miss Hazel M Wood's Charitable Trust
The Worshipful Company of Painter-Stainers
and others who wish to remain anonymous

AMERICAN ASSOCIATES OF THE ROYAL ACADEMY TRUST
Major Benefactors
Mr Walter Fitch
Mr Donald Kahn
Mr James Slaughter

Benjamin West Society
Mrs Walter Annenberg
Mr Edwin Cox
Mr Francis Finlay III
Mrs Kathleen Ford

Benefactors
Mr Hamish Maxwell III
The Honorable John Whitehead
Mr Frederick Whittemore

Sponsors
Mr Herbert Adler
Mrs Jan Cowles
Mrs Katherine Findlay
Mrs Henry Heinz
Mr David Hockney
Mr James Kemper
Mrs Lucy McGrath
Ms Diane Nixon
Mr John Robinson
Mr Arthur Sulzberger
Mr Vernon Taylor, Jr

Patrons
Ms Helen Abell
Ms Britt Allcroft
Mr Steven Ausnit
Mr E Aylward
Mrs A Barlow Ferguson
Ms Robin Bell
Mr Donald Best II
Mr Henry Breyer, Jr
Mrs Mildred Brinn, Jr
Dr Robert Carroll
Mr Benjamin Coates
Anne Davidson
Ms Zita Davisson

Mrs Charles Dyson, Jr
Mr Jonathan Farkas
Mrs Robert Ferst
Mr Richard Ford, Jr
Ms Barbara Fox-Bordiga, Jr
Mrs Betty Gordon
Mrs Lee Granger
Mrs Rachel Grody
Mr Irving Harris
Mr Gurnee Hart
Mr Gustave Hauser
Dr Bruce Horten
Mrs Mary Hyde
Mr Robert Irwin
The Honorable W Johnston
Mr William Karatz
Mrs George Kaufman
Mrs Stephen Kellen
Mr Michael Kempner
Mr Gary Kraut
The Honorable Philip Lader
Mrs Katherine Lawrence
Mr Arthur Loeb
Ms Barbara Missett
Mrs Garrett Moran
Mr Paul Morgan
Mr Paul Myers
Mr Wilson Nolen
Mr Robert Peterson
Mr Jeffrey Pettit
Ms Barbara Pine
Mr Claude du Pont
Dr James Reibel
Mrs Virginia Ridder
Ambassador Enriquillo del Rosario
Ms Louisa Sarofim
Mrs Frances Scaife
Mr Stanley Scott
Mr Albert Small
Mr Art Soares
Mr Morton Sosland
Mr Stephen Stamas
Mr Richard Steinwurtzel
Ms Brenda Straus
Mr Martin Sullivan
Mrs Royce Tate
Ms Britt Tidelius
Mr Lewis Townsend
Mrs Richard Tullis
Mrs Vincent Villard
Mrs William Weaver
Mr George White
Dr Robert Wickham
Mr Robert Wilson, Jr
Miss Diane Wolf

Donors
Mrs Lester Anderson
Mr James Armstrong
Mr Tobin Armstrong
Mr Stephen Bechtel
Mr W Blackhurst
Mr Geoffrey Bradfield
Mrs Edgar Brenner
The Hon John Calkins
Mr Philip Carroll
Ms Jayne Chase
Mr Reginald Collier
Mr Richard Colyear, Jr
Mrs Yvonne Connors
Ms Marian Davis
Mr Paul Feeney
Mrs Laurence Fell
Mr Ralph Fields
Mr Christopher Forbes
Mrs Raymond Foster
Mr Helmut Friedlaender
Mr Gerald Gehman III
Mr Gordon Getty
Mr Alfred Glassell
Mr Ralph Golby
Mr Ellis Goodman
Mr Jas Gundry

Mr O Harrison
Mrs Judith Heath
Mr C Hugh Hildesley
Ms Jessie Jamar
Dr Attallah Kappas
Mr Herbert Kasper
Mr Nicholas Kirkbride
The Hon Samuel Lessey
Mr Henry Lynn
Mrs Sue McMurrey
Ms Helen Mavrophilippas
Mrs Anne Miller
Mrs Joan Navin
Mrs Charles Olson
Ms Cordella Owens, Jr
Mrs Carol Parsons
Mrs Frances Philipp
Mr Max Pine
Mr Robert Pirie
Ms Alice Pollner
Mr Howard Ross
Mr William Rothacker
Mrs Peter Rowley
Mrs Signe Ruddock
Ms Rosita Sarnoff
Mr Stuart Scott
Ms Charlotte Sickles
Ms Muriel Siebert
Mrs Martin Slifka
Mrs Cullen Smith
Ms Kathleen Smith
Mr Robert Snyder
Ms Adrienne Southworth
Dr Richard Stark
Ms Patricia Sullivan
Ms Evelyn Tompkins
Ms Linda Webb, Jr
Mrs Claire Whelan
Ms Shelby White
Mrs Walter Wilds

Supporters
Mrs Vincent Astor
Mr Innis Bromfield
Ms Elizabeth Goldsmith
Dr George Heyer
Mr John Hupper, Jr
Mrs Mary Mulcahy
The Lord Renwick of Clifton
Ms Emily Scheuer
Sir John Weston
Mrs Eleanor Wood Prince, Sr

Junior Memberships
Mr John Fiorilla
Ms Jennifer Powers
Miss Felicia Taylor
and others who wish to remain anonymous